THE
PALEO DIET
MADE EASY

THE PALEO DIET

LOVED BY CELEBRITIES & ATHLETES ALIKE

EAT LIKE YOUR ANCESTORS TO LOSE WEIGHT & GET FIT

MADE EASY

SIMPLE INGREDIENTS

NO JUNK → NO STARVING

OVER 100 RECIPES

JOY SKIPPER

hamlyn

An Hachette UK Company
www.hachette.co.uk

First published in Great Britain in 2014 by
Hamlyn, a division of Octopus Publishing Group Ltd
Endeavour House, 189 Shaftesbury Avenue, London, WC2H 8JY
www.octopusbooks.co.uk

An Hachette UK Company
www.hachette.co.uk

Distributed in the US by Hachette Book Group
1290 Avenue of the Americas, 4th and 5th Floors, New York, NY 10020

Distributed in Canada by Canadian Manda Group
664 Annette St.
Toronto, Ontario, Canada M6S 2C8

Joy Skipper asserts the moral right to be identified as the author of this work

ISBN 978-0-600-62985-6

A CIP catalogue record for this book is available from the British Library

Printed and bound by CPI Group (UK) Ltd, Croydon, CR0 4YY

10 9 8 7 6 5 4 3 2 1

Commissioning Editor: Eleanor Maxfield
Managing Editor: Clare Churly
Designer: Eoghan O'Brien
Design: Jeremy Tilston
Production Controller: Allison Gonsalves

NOTES:
Standard level spoon and cup measureds are used in all recipes.

Ovens should be preheated to the specified temperature. If using a convection oven, follow
the manufacturer's instructions for adjusting the time and temperature. Broilers should also
be preheated.

This book includes dishes made with nuts and nut derivatives. It is advisable for those
with known allergic reactions to nuts and nut derivatives and those who may be potentially
vulnerable to these allergies, such as pregnant and nursing mothers, people with weakened
immune systems, the elderly, babies, and children, to avoid dishes made with nuts and nut oils.

The U.S. Food and Drug Administration advises that eggs should not be consumed raw. This book
contains some dishes made with raw or lightly cooked eggs. It is prudent for more vulnerable
people, such as pregnant and nursing mothers, people with weakened immune systems, the
elderly, babies, and young children to avoid uncooked or lightly cooked dishes made with eggs.

CONTENTS

The Paleo Diet 7

1. Breakfasts 19

2. Soups 27

3. Salads 37

4. Fish and Seafood 55

5. Meat, Poultry, and Game 85

6. Vegetarian 109

7. Snacks 115

8. Sweet Stuff 129

9. Drinks 145

Index 154

THE PALEO DIET

INTRODUCTION

This book will introduce you to the concept of the diet believed to have been eaten by our ancestors thousands of years ago, enabling them to stay lean and healthy. The book explains the basics of the diet, plus gives plenty of tips and ideas to help you get started, and it includes more than a hundred recipes to incorporate into your everyday life.

The Paleolithic diet (known as the Paleo diet) is often referred to as the hunter-gatherer diet and includes any food that could be hunted or found, such as meats, fish, nuts, leafy greens, and seeds. It is based on the concept that the best diet is the one to which we are genetically adapted, with the premise that human genetics have hardly changed since the dawn of agriculture, and on research showing that the aged populations of hunter-gatherer societies were virtually free of high cholesterol, diabetes, obesity, hypertension, and other chronic diseases that have become endemic in Western societies. There are signs that indicate our modern diet full of refined foods, trans fats, and sugar is the root of most degenerative diseases, including cancer and heart disease, depression, and fertility problems. We have changed our diets, but our genetics have not changed enough to accommodate them.

Over the past couple of years, a number of authors have written about the Paleo diet, each with their own variation. It's difficult for us to know for certain what Paleo people ate or how they lived, but in essence the Paleo diet is based around a much more nutrient-dense, toxin-free, whole-food diet than that which is currently being eaten today. The best way to think of this diet is as a particular approach to eating, with a template that can be adjusted to suit each individual's biochemical needs. It is also important to think of it not so much as a diet but as a healthy eating plan that can be maintained for life.

HOW TO USE THE BOOK

The great thing about the Paleo diet is that once you know what you can and cannot eat, there is nothing else to worry about. No calorie counting, no measuring of foods—the foods you are allowed can be eaten as often as you desire. The only foods that need to be limited are root vegetables and fruit (see page 17), because these are high in starch and sugar, and if excess sugar is not burned off, it turns into fat.

This book provides you with recipes featuring only the allowed foods, and these can be used to make meals and snacks throughout the day. The recipes will give you ideas of ways to use the many foods available on the Paleo diet—as long as you adhere to those foods, you can also experiment with your own recipes, too.

So what can you eat? Anything that the hunter-gatherer would have been able to forage for—meats (Paleolithic man would have found wild meat, so the leanest cuts you can find are best), fish and seafood, vegetables, fruits, eggs, nuts, and seeds. You may also reduce your toxin intake by choosing nutrient-dense organic foods. Foods to avoid include all grains, legumes (such as beans and peas), dairy, and refined sugars (see page 12).

The Paleo diet is a diet that can be followed for life, not just as a short-term weight-loss plan. It is a healthy, long-term eating plan that has been shown to reduce a number of modern diseases.

IS THE PALEO DIET FOR EVERYONE?

There is no such thing as an optimal diet for the whole world—think of the diet of the Inuit or Masai, who eat high-fat diets yet remain healthy. So it's important to remember that our ancestors didn't all eat the same diet—there was a wide variation in the proportion of protein, carbohydrate, and fat consumed, and the different types of food consumed by different populations around the world.

We are all individual, with individual lifestyles, and we grew up in different environments, with different toxin exposure and different experiences, so many of our genes are the same, but some are different, and the way some of them may have been expressed may also be different. So the Paleo diet is about finding a diet that works for you.

If you have been on a diet that was based on a lot of processed food for many years, along with high alcohol and toxin intake, the transition to a nutrient-dense, low-toxic diet may not be a smooth one. This doesn't mean that the Paleo diet is not for you, it may just mean you have some work to do on your digestive system or other systems in the body, to be sure that you are digesting and detoxifying optimally. There is no such thing as a quick fix, especially if you have been on a heavily processed food diet for a long time.

Two groups of people that may struggle with this diet are vegetarians and vegans as, being based on a hunter-gatherer diet, it includes meat, poultry, fish, and eggs. And without legumes and grains, vegetarians and vegans will not be able to sustain a balanced diet with enough protein intake.

HOW DOES THE DIET WORK?

A Paleo diet is naturally lower in carbohydrate than the modern diet and automatically eliminates many foods that are low in nutrients and high in calories. It will also eliminate processed foods that are high in hidden sugars, fats, and toxins, and it will reduce the intake of foods that may cause intolerances or allergies, or foods that may be hard to digest. The carbohydrates on the Paleo diet (fruit and vegetables) are also low on the glycemic index, meaning that they cause slow and limited rises in your blood sugar and insulin levels. Your body's blood sugar balance may be improved, because you will be eating more protein and good fat that will sustain your appetite for longer.

HEALTH BENEFITS

There are a number of reasons why this diet is healthy, some of which have already been mentioned, including cutting out toxins and increasing your intake of nutrient-dense foods.

When you consider that the body is made up of protein, carbohydrates, and fats, it makes sense that if you feed your body those nutrients in the cleanest form possible, it will perform better.

By eliminating processed foods, you are automatically eating a low-sodium diet while increasing your intake of potassium (rich in many vegetables, nuts, and seeds), and the combination of low sodium and high potassium is a recipe for good vascular health and low blood pressure.

Clinical trials have shown that the Paleo diet may lower the risk of cardiovascular disease, blood pressure, and markers of inflammation; help with weight loss; reduce acne; and promote optimum health and athletic performance.

THE PALEO DIET AND EXERCISE

As with all healthy eating plans, you will see better results if you are active. Hunter-gatherers were physically active on a daily basis, while they were seeking food, water, and shelter. We no longer have to do these things, but getting regular exercise may be beneficial both for weight loss and long-term health.

If you are intending to follow the Paleo diet and have not been getting regular exercise, seek help from a healthcare professional to be assessed for the level of exercise you should start with.

If you are a training athlete, you will no doubt be wondering if this diet will suit you. Not so long ago, carbohydrates were the endurance nutrient of choice, and protein was the focus of all body builders and strength athletes, but things have moved on since then. The Paleo diet is naturally high in animal protein, which is the richest source of branched-chain amino acids, needed for building and repairing muscles. It also reduces muscle loss because it is an alkaline diet (one way the body neutralizes an acid-producing diet is by breaking down muscle). The high intake of vegetables and fruit also ensures a high intake of vitamins, minerals, and phytochemicals, which help to support the immune system, an important issue for all athletes.

WHAT TO EXPECT ON THE DIET

If your present diet is high in processed foods, coffee, alcohol, wheat, and dairy, it may take you a while to adjust to your new diet and to find the foods that work for you. Keeping a food diary from day one may be helpful with this, because it's hard to remember how you felt and if any foods affected you in any way.

You may also get withdrawal symptoms from cutting out some of the old foods, so it could be a while before you start to feel better and see your body shape change.

GETTING STARTED

If you find the thought of a "diet" somewhat daunting, set yourself a time challenge to start with. Commit to a 30-day period where you eliminate the foods suggested below, therefore reducing toxins and food sensitivities, and so reducing allergic reactions, and introduce the new foods that may have been absent from your diet, which may hopefully improve digestion, boost energy, regulate sugar balance, and normalize weight. Once you start to get to grips with your new eating plan, you may find some foods agree with you more than others, so you can start to tailor the diet to suit your individual needs.

Here is a basic list of foods to eat and not eat:

Eat:
- Grass-produced meats (grain causes the same problem in animals as it does in humans)
- Fish (wild is best to avoid mercury and other toxins found in farmed fish)
- Seafood
- Fresh fruit (limit the amount if you are trying to lose weight, because it is high in natural sugar)
- Fresh vegetables
- Eggs (look for omega-3 enriched)
- Nuts
- Seeds
- Healthy oil—olive, flaxseed, avocado, coconut, walnut

Don't eat:
- Legumes such as beans and peas (including peanuts)
- Dairy
- Cereal grains
- Refined sugar
- Potatoes
- Processed foods
- Salt

HINTS AND TIPS FOR BEGINNERS

Adhering to a new eating plan can be difficult when there are outside influences, such as work or family, to juggle, too, so the following hints and tips may be useful:

- **Set small, achievable targets**—try including a new food each week or increasing your exercise by walking to a farther bus stop each morning.

- **Get support**—get your family or friends involved by asking them to join you on the diet. That way, if you are cooking for the whole family, you won't have to make separate meals, and everyone will benefit!

- **Don't get hungry**—be sure that you plan your day with enough healthy snacks that mean you never get hungry; eating little and often is fine as long as it is based on the foods you are allowed. Maintain your appetite throughout the day, which will also help to keep your blood sugar balanced, causing less stress on the body. The less hungry you are, the easier it is to lose weight!

- **Be aware of what you are eating**—don't fall into the trap of "mindless eating," just eating because food is there or has been offered. Eat in a conscious way, and savor each mouthful.

- **Personalize the diet to suit you**—it may take a few weeks for you to get to know which foods you like and which suit you. You also have your own routine and it's important to make your diet work around that.

- **Make changes that are sustainable**—gradually change your diet to suit you, and make sure the changes you make are those that can be maintained for life, not just for a few weeks.

10 WAYS TO MAKE THE PALEO DIET WORK FOR YOU

1

BE ORGANIZED

Spend time at the beginning of the week to shop and prepare food for the week ahead.

2

PLAN AHEAD

Plan your meals in advance so you have something tasty to look forward to, so that you don't get hungry and reach for the wrong foods.

3

TAKE FOODS WITH YOU

If you work away from home, make yourself delicious lunches to take with you.

4

RESTOCK THE PANTRY AND REFRIGERATOR

Only have Paleo foods in the house; that way, you won't have temptations that can lead to you cheating.

5

FRESH PRODUCE DELIVERY

Sign up to a fresh produce delivery plan from a local farm in your Community Supported Agriculture (CSA) network to be sure you are eating fresh organic vegetables each week. You may even get to try some new ones you didn't know you liked.

6

KEEP IT SIMPLE

With each meal or snack, first include protein (meat, poultry, fish, or eggs), then add some vegetables or fruit.

7

EAT REGULARLY

Don't let yourself get hungry. Eat little and often; having snacks, such as a small handful of nuts and seeds with a piece of fruit, will sustain you between meals.

8

EAT A RAINBOW!

Vegetables are loaded with essential vitamins, minerals, enzymes, antioxidants, fiber, and water, all essential for optimum health. The color of your fruit and vegetables is linked to the nutrients they include, so eat as many colorful fruit and vegetables a day as you can—variety is key.

9

USE THE 80:20 RULE

If you find you have a day or night when you really cannot follow the diet (for example, you are invited out to dinner), don't worry; just count it as your 20 percent of being non-Paleo for that week, and get right back onto the Paleo eating plan the next day.

10

START A FOOD DIARY

Keep a note of what you eat, how you feel and how you sleep. Hopefully, over time you will see positive changes and may be able to relate them to foods you are consuming.

FREQUENTLY ASKED QUESTIONS

• •

Can a vegetarian or vegan follow the Paleo diet?
As the Paleo diet is based on what a hunter-gatherer would have caught/found, it naturally includes meat. It is important to include protein in the diet, which most vegetarians or vegans would gain from eating legumes and cereals, but these foods contain antinutrients that may have a negative effect (see below).

Is it suitable for children?
If you can get your child to eat enough vegetables, this diet is fine—children really don't need all the refined carbohydrates (pizza, pasta, etc.) to enable them to grow, because they can get carbohydrates (along with fiber, vitamins, and minerals) from vegetables.

Is it suitable during pregnancy?
Because the diet is rich in fresh fruit, vegetables, organic meat, and fish, it is fine to follow during pregnancy.

How will I get my intake of calcium for my bones without dairy?
Bone health is mainly dependent on an acid/alkaline dietary balance. If the acid in the body is too high, then calcium is "pulled" from the bones to neutralize it. Acid-producing foods include cheese, grains, legumes, and salted foods. Fruit and vegetables are alkaline, so increasing these in your diet should bring the acid/alkaline and, therefore, the calcium back into balance. Leafy green vegetables, such as kale, and some nuts (almonds) and seeds (sesame) are also rich in calcium.

Is organic food really better for you?
There is always plenty of debate about this, but research has shown that foods that have had to battle the elements to survive and grow without the help of pesticides and fertilizers are probably more nutrient-dense than those that had help.

Will I lose weight on the Paleo diet?

If your present diet has been high in processed foods and refined carbohydrates, there is a good chance that you may lose weight, because you will be eating foods that are easier for the body to recognize and digest.

How much fruit can I eat on the diet?

In general, fresh fruits are healthy foods that are good sources of minerals, vitamins, and fiber. However, the fruits we eat today are sweeter, larger, and contain less fiber than their wild counterparts, so if you are trying to lose weight, it may be beneficial to limit high-sugar fruits, such as bananas, mangoes, grapes, apples, pineapples, and kiwifruit, and try to include more vegetables in your diet instead. Root vegetables, however, are higher in starch and sugar than leafy green vegetables, and so they should be eaten in moderation, too.

Why no beans?

Beans contain lectins, which are carbohydrate-binding proteins present in most plants, especially seeds, beans, and tubers, such as cereals, potatoes, and beans. Until recently, their main use was as histology and blood transfusion reagents, but in the past two decades it has been realized that many lectins are toxic and inflammatory.

Which oils are allowed on the Paleo diet?

There are many different views on the kinds of oils that should be consumed when following the Paleo diet. The consensus, however, seems to be that oils from all the plants that are allowed can be consumed: olive oil (great for salads and sautéing, but don't heat too high); coconut oil (high in saturated fats but withstands high cooking temperatures so good for stir-fries); avocado oil (delicious in salad dressings or cooking at low temperatures); and sesame oil (rich in flavor, so only a small amount is needed, but it is not recommended as an everyday oil). Oils that should not be used are those rich in omega-6 fatty acids, plus oils from legumes, soy, etc. (peanut oil, vegetable oil, sunflower oil, corn oil, canola oil).

What can I drink and use instead of milk?
Almond milk and coconut milk.

Can I eat peanuts on the Paleo diet?
No, they are legumes.

Is alcohol allowed on the diet?
Alcohol is not allowed on the diet, although if you occasionally add wine to food when you are cooking, just be sure to burn off the alcohol.

Is the Paleo diet expensive?
The diet does not have to be expensive, especially if you normally buy prepared food—cooking from scratch is not only healthier, but cheaper, too. Shop around to get the best prices, buy from local markets, and maybe even think about growing your own organic vegetables!

Can I get most of the ingredients at a supermarket?
Yes, all Paleo foods are readily available in supermarkets, including the fresh ingredients. If you have a good butcher and fish dealer nearby, you may also want to visit them to see what offers they have and get advice about cooking the best cuts of meat or fresh fish.

Any tips for what to grab on the run?
Nuts, seeds, and fruit are the easiest foods to carry around.

1

BREAKFASTS

SMOKED HADDOCK SCRAMBLED EGGS

This protein-rich breakfast sets you up for a busy day.

SERVES 2
PREPARATION TIME 10 MINUTES
COOKING TIME 12 MINUTES

1 bay leaf
1 thyme sprig
1 garlic clove
4 whole peppercorns
⅔ cup nondairy milk
4 oz smoked haddock fillet or other smoked fish
4 extra-large eggs, beaten
2 tablespoons chopped chives
freshly ground black pepper

1 Place the bay leaf, thyme, garlic, peppercorns, and milk in a saucepan and slowly bring to a simmer. Add the smoked haddock, turn off the heat, and let stand for 6 minutes.

2 Remove the haddock from the poaching liquid and flake into large pieces, discarding the skin and any bones. Reserve 2 tablespoons of the poaching liquid.

3 Heat a nonstick saucepan over low heat, add the eggs, and cook for a few minutes, stirring occasionally, until just scrambled, then add the haddock and reserved poaching liquid and cook for another minute.

4 Stir in the chives, season with black pepper, and serve immediately.

CHORIZO AND EGG-TOPPED BAKED MUSHROOMS

• •

Chorizo has a distinct taste and the mushrooms bring out the best of its flavor.

• •

SERVES 2
PREPARATION TIME 10 MINUTES
COOKING TIME 15–17 MINUTES

2 large portobello mushrooms,
   cleaned, stems removed
   and chopped
1 tablespoon olive oil
1 oz chorizo sausage, sliced
2 scallions, sliced
1½ cups sliced small button
   mushrooms
1 tablespoon chopped parsley
2 eggs
freshly ground black pepper

1 Place the portobello mushrooms on a baking sheet, gill sides up, and drizzle with half the oil. Bake in a preheated oven, at 400°F, for 15 minutes.

2 Meanwhile, heat the remaining oil in a skillet, add the chorizo, and cook for 3–4 minutes. Add the scallions and cook for another 2–3 minutes, until softened. Add the sliced button mushrooms and chopped stems and continue to cook for 8–10 minutes. Stir in half the parsley.

3 Toward the end of the cooking time, poach the eggs in a separate small saucepan of simmering water for 3–5 minutes, or until cooked to your preference.

4 Divide the chorizo mixture among the mushrooms and top each one with a poached egg.

5 Season with black pepper, sprinkle with the remaining parsley, and serve.

HUEVOS RANCHEROS

A traditional Mexican farming dish, this is a delicious way to serve eggs in the morning. If you want a little more spice, just add a finely diced red chile to the pepper mixture, too.

SERVES 4
PREPARATION TIME 10 MINUTES
COOKING TIME 15 MINUTES

3 tablespoons olive oil
1 large onion, diced
2 red bell peppers, cored,
    seeded, and diced
2 garlic cloves, crushed
¾ teaspoon dried oregano
2 (14½ oz) cans diced tomatoes
4 eggs
pinch of smoked paprika
1 tablespoon chopped parsley,
    to garnish

1 Heat 2 tablespoons of the oil in a skillet, add the onion, red bell peppers, garlic, and oregano and sauté for 5 minutes, until softened.

2 Add the tomatoes and cook for another 5 minutes, then pour into a shallow ovenproof dish and keep warm.

3 Heat the remaining oil in a large clean skillet, add the eggs, and fry until the whites are set and the yolks are cooked to your preference.

4 Serve the eggs on top of the tomato sauce, sprinkled with the smoked paprika and parsley.

BREAKFAST TORTILLA

Tortillas are simple to make, and you can add any vegetables of your choice. Prepare in advance and serve in wedges for breakfast, or wrap them up for a perfect packed lunch.

SERVES 4
PREPARATION TIME 10 MINUTES
COOKING TIME 25–30 MINUTES

2 tablespoons olive oil
2 shallots, diced
4 bacon slices, fat removed
   and chopped
4 cups sliced cremini mushrooms
6 extra-large eggs
8 cherry tomatoes, halved
1 tablespoon chopped parsley
freshly ground black pepper

1 Heat 1 tablespoon of the oil in a skillet with a flameproof handle, add the shallots and bacon, and cook for 3–4 minutes, until the shallots have softened. Add the mushrooms and cook for another 5–6 minutes, until soft. Remove the mixture with a slotted spoon and set aside.

2 Beat the eggs in a large bowl and season with black pepper, then stir in the bacon mixture, tomatoes, and parsley.

3 Heat the remaining oil in the skillet over high heat, pour in the egg mixture, and cook for 1–2 minutes. Reduce the temperature to low and cook for another 12–15 minutes, keeping an eye on the edges to make sure it is not overcooked underneath— the top should still be runny.

4 Place the pan under a preheated broiler and cook the top until golden and bubbling. To turn out, place a plate on top of the tortilla and carefully turn the pan upside down. Serve the tortilla hot or cold, cut into wedges.

BAKED EGGS WITH SPINACH AND HAM

This is a great weekend breakfast treat.
If you want to spice it up, add a finely diced
red chile to the tomato mixture.

SERVES 2
PREPARATION TIME 10 MINUTES
COOKING TIME 25 MINUTES

1 tablespoon olive oil
1 onion, diced
1 garlic clove, crushed
1 (14½ oz) can diced tomatoes
½ cup water
½ cup sliced roasted peppers,
   homemade or from a jar
6 oz lean ham, shredded
2 cups baby spinach leaves
2 eggs
pinch of smoked paprika
freshly ground black pepper

1 Heat the oil in an ovenproof skillet, add the onion, and cook for 4–5 minutes, until softened. Add the garlic and cook for another minute.

2 Pour in the tomatoes and measured water and season with black pepper, then stir in the roasted peppers and ham. Bring to a simmer and cook for 10 minutes.

3 Stir in the spinach and, when it starts to wilt, make 2 hollows in the sauce. Crack an egg into each hollow and sprinkle with a pinch of paprika.

4 Transfer to a preheated oven, at 350°F, for 10 minutes, or until the egg whites have set.

DIPPY EGG WITH ASPARAGUS SPEARS

Asparagus and eggs are a perfect combination, so why not try them for breakfast or brunch?

SERVES 1
PREPARATION TIME 5 MINUTES,
  PLUS COOLING
COOKING TIME 6–8 MINUTES

1 tablespoon hazelnuts
4–5 asparagus spears,
  woody ends snapped off
1 extra-large egg

1 Heat a dry, nonstick skillet over medium-low heat and dry-fry the hazelnuts for 3–4 minutes, shaking the pan occasionally, until golden brown and toasted. Let cool slightly, then chop and set aside.

2 Cook the asparagus in a large saucepan of boiling water for 3–4 minutes, until just tender.

3 Meanwhile, in a separate small saucepan, boil the egg in boiling water for 3–4 minutes, until soft-boiled.

4 Drain the asparagus, place on a warmed plate, and sprinkle with the chopped hazelnuts.

5 Place the egg in an eggcup on the same plate and serve.

BREAKFAST BANANA SPLIT

Banana splits usually includes ice cream, but this wonderful breakfast will get you off to a healthy start instead.

SERVES 2
PREPARATION TIME 5 MINUTES
COOKING TIME 4–5 MINUTES

1 tablespoon coconut oil
1 tablespoon honey
2 bananas, halved lengthwise
2 tablespoons slivered almonds
¼ cup walnuts
1 orange
1 sweet apple, grated

1 Heat the oil and honey in a skillet until melted and sizzling. Add the bananas, cut side down, and cook for 3–4 minutes, until golden.

2 Meanwhile, heat a separate dry, nonstick skillet over medium-low heat, add the slivered almonds and walnuts, and dry-fry for 3–4 minutes, shaking the pan occasionally, until golden brown and toasted.

3 Grate the zest of the orange into a bowl, then, using a sharp knife, remove the peel and pith from the orange. Cut out the segments and add to the bowl with the grated apple. Mix together.

4 Spoon the bananas onto 4 warmed plates and top with the apple and orange mixture. Sprinkle with the toasted nuts and serve drizzled with the juices from the pan.

② SOUPS

SALMON AND HORSERADISH SOUP

The creaminess of the salmon and the heat of the horseradish go really well together in this soup.

SERVES 4
PREPARATION TIME 15 MINUTES
COOKING TIME 30 MINUTES

1 small head of cauliflower,
  broken into florets
1 tablespoon olive oil
1 onion, chopped
1 leek, trimmed, cleaned,
  and shredded
2 cups peeled and diced rutabaga
5 cups fish stock
2 tomatoes, chopped
1 lb skinless salmon fillet,
  cut into large chunks
½ cup nondairy milk
1 teaspoon grated fresh
  horseradish
juice of ½ lemon
1 small bunch of dill,
  coarsely chopped
freshly ground black pepper

1 Cook the cauliflower in a saucepan of boiling water for 4–5 minutes, until just tender. Drain and set aside.

2 Meanwhile, heat the oil in a separate large saucepan, add the onion and leek, and sauté for 3–4 minutes, until softened. Add the rutabaga and cook for another 2 minutes.

3 Pour in the stock and bring to a boil, then reduce the heat, cover, and simmer for 10 minutes. Add the tomatoes and drained cauliflower and cook for another 4–5 minutes.

4 Gently stir in the salmon and cook for 5 minutes, or until just cooked through.

5 Stir in the milk, horseradish, and lemon juice and bring to a simmer, then sprinkle in the dill and season with black pepper. Ladle the soup into warmed bowls and serve.

SMOKED HADDOCK AND CORN CHOWDER

The chowder can also be made with smoked cod or even thick chunks of smoked salmon.

SERVES 4
PREPARATION TIME 10 MINUTES
COOKING TIME 10–12 MINUTES

1 tablespoon olive oil
1 onion, chopped
2 celery sticks, sliced
2 cups frozen or canned
    corn kernels
2½ cups vegetable stock
2½ cups nondairy milk
12 oz smoked haddock or halibut
    fillet, skinned and cut into
    bite-size pieces
1 tablespoon chopped parsley,
    to garnish

1 Heat the oil in a saucepan, add the onion and celery, and sauté for 4–5 minutes, until softened. Add the corn kernels and cook, stirring, for 2 minutes.

2 Pour in the stock and milk and bring to a boil, then add the fish and simmer for 4–5 minutes, or until the fish is cooked through.

3 Ladle the soup into warmed bowls and serve sprinkled with the parsley.

ROASTED TOMATO AND GARLIC SOUP

Roasting tomatoes before using them for soup brings out their natural sweetness.

SERVES 4
PREPARATION TIME 10 MINUTES
COOKING TIME 25 MINUTES

8 ripe tomatoes (about 2 lb), halved
4 garlic cloves, unpeeled
2 tablespoons olive oil
1 onion, chopped
1 carrot, peeled and chopped
1 celery stick, sliced
1 red bell pepper, cored, seeded, and chopped
3 cups hot vegetable stock
freshly ground black pepper

1 Place the tomato halves and garlic cloves in a roasting pan. Sprinkle with 1 tablespoon of the oil and season with black pepper. Roast in a preheated oven, at 400°F, for 20 minutes.

2 Halfway through the tomato cooking time, heat the remaining oil in a saucepan, add the onion, carrot, celery, and red bell pepper, and sauté over low heat for 10 minutes, until softened.

3 Remove the garlic cloves from the roasted tomatoes and squeeze the garlic flesh into the saucepan with the sautéed vegetables, then add the roasted tomatoes and all the juices and stir in the stock.

4 Using a handheld immersion blender, blend the soup until smooth. Reheat to a simmer, then ladle the soup into warmed bowls and serve.

LEEK AND ARUGULA SOUP

A simple and quick way to make soup, which works equally well with watercress if you happen to have some on hand.

SERVES 4
PREPARATION TIME 5 MINUTES
COOKING TIME 14–18 MINUTES

1 tablespoon olive oil
6 leeks, trimmed, cleaned, and sliced
2 cups hot vegetable stock
2¼ cups arugula leaves
1 cup nondairy milk
freshly ground black pepper

1 Heat the oil in a saucepan, add the leeks, and sauté for 8-10 minutes, until softened.

2 Add the stock and arugula leaves. Simmer for 4–6 minutes, then add the milk.

3 Using a handheld immersion blender, blend the soup until smooth. Reheat to a simmer and season with black pepper. Ladle the soup into warmed bowls and serve.

ONION SOUP

Traditional French onion soup takes a while to make, but it is worth the effort. Letting the onions caramelize slowly gives the soup an intense, sweet flavor.

SERVES 4
PREPARATION TIME 10 MINUTES
COOKING TIME 45–50 MINUTES

1 tablespoon olive oil
6 yellow onions (about 2 lb),
    thinly sliced
2 tablespoons thyme leaves
5 cups beef stock
freshly ground black pepper

1 Heat the oil in a saucepan, add the onions and thyme leaves, and cook over low heat for 18–20 minutes, until the onions are soft. Increase the heat and cook for another 15–18 minutes, stirring occasionally, until the onions darken and start to caramelize.

2 Pour in the stock and bring to a boil, then reduce the heat and simmer for 10 minutes. Season with black pepper, then ladle the soup into warmed bowls and serve.

3 Alternatively, to let the flavor develop, the soup can be cooled, then stored in the refrigerator for 24 hours before reheating.

GAZPACHO

Gazpacho is a wonderful summer soup, made when all the seasonal ingredients are at their best—use the ripest ingredients you can find.

SERVES 4
PREPARATION TIME 15 MINUTES

4 scallions, chopped
2 garlic cloves
1 red bell pepper, cored, seeded, and chopped
½ cucumber
16 ripe roma or plum tomatoes (about 2 lb), halved
juice of 1 lemon
3 tablespoons olive oil

TO SERVE
1 hard-boiled egg, shelled and chopped
1 avocado, pitted, peeled, and chopped

1 Place the scallions, garlic, and red bell pepper in a food processor or blender and process until broken down. Add the cucumber, tomatoes, and lemon juice and process again.

2 Add 2 tablespoons of the oil and blend to your preferred consistency (you can make this soup as smooth or chunky as desired).

3 Pour into 4 bowls, then top with the chopped egg and avocado and a drizzle of the remaining oil. Serve immediately.

CHILLED AVOCADO SOUP WITH RED PEPPER SALSA

This cold, creamy soup is ideal for a summer's day. And it is rich in essential fats, too.

SERVES 4
PREPARATION TIME 15 MINUTES,
PLUS CHILLING
COOKING TIME 2–3 MINUTES

4 large avocados
juice of 1 lime
½ red chile, seeded and
   finely diced
3¾ cups vegetable stock, chilled
freshly ground black pepper
ice cubes, to serve

FOR THE SALSA
2 tablespoons pumpkin seeds
2 scallions, finely sliced
½ red bell pepper, cored, seeded,
   and diced
¼ cucumber, diced
1 tablespoon cilantro leaves
2 tablespoons olive oil
2 teaspoons lemon juice

1 Halve, pit, and peel the avocados, then coarsely chop the flesh and put into a food processor or blender with the lime juice, chile, and stock. Blend until smooth, then season with black pepper and chill for 15 minutes.

2 Meanwhile, heat a dry, nonstick skillet over medium-low heat and dry-fry the pumpkin seeds for 2–3 minutes, shaking the pan occasionally, until golden brown and toasted. Let cool.

3 To make the salsa, place the toasted pumpkin seeds in a bowl, add the remaining ingredients, and mix together.

4 Place a couple of ice cubes in each of 4 shallow bowls, then pour the soup over them. Spoon the salsa over the soup and serve immediately.

TOMATO, SAFFRON, AND ALMOND SOUP

This unusual combination of ingredients makes a warming, tasty soup.

SERVES 4
PREPARATION TIME 5 MINUTES
COOKING TIME 35–40 MINUTES

1 tablespoon olive oil
1 onion, chopped
1 garlic clove, crushed
2 (14½ oz) cans diced tomatoes
4 cups vegetable stock
big pinch of saffron threads
¾ cup ground almonds
   (almond meal)
freshly ground black pepper

1 Heat the oil in a saucepan, add the onion and garlic, and cook for 4–5 minutes, until softened.

2 Add the tomatoes, stock, and saffron and bring to a boil, then reduce the heat and simmer for 25–30 minutes.

3 Stir in the ground almonds and season with black pepper, then cook for another 5 minutes, until starting to thicken.

4 Using a handheld immersion blender, blend the soup until smooth. Reheat to a simmer, then ladle the soup into warmed bowls and serve.

3

SALADS

SPINACH AND SALMON SALAD WITH ARUGULA PESTO

Pesto is usually made with basil leaves, but there is no reason why you can't use other herbs or greens, such as arugula or parsley.

SERVES 4
PREPARATION TIME 10 MINUTES
COOKING TIME 6–8 MINUTES

4 salmon fillets, about 5 oz each
1 tablespoon extra-virgin olive oil
1 (12 oz) package baby
  spinach leaves
3 tablespoons pine nuts
juice of 1 lemon

FOR THE PESTO
3½ cups arugula leaves
1 garlic clove
3 tablespoons pine nuts
¼ cup extra-virgin olive oil

1 To make the pesto, put the arugula, garlic, and pine nuts into a food processor or blender and process until broken down. With the motor still running, slowly add the oil through the feeder tube until it forms a loose paste. Set aside.

2 Cook the salmon under a preheated hot broiler for 3–4 minutes on each side, until the fish is cooked through.

3 Meanwhile, heat the oil in a skillet, add the spinach, and cook until just lightly wilted. Turn off the heat.

4 Flake the salmon into large pieces, discarding the skin and any bones, and place in a large salad bowl. Add the spinach and arugula pesto and toss together. Sprinkle with the pine nuts and serve drizzled with the lemon juice.

SESAME SEARED TUNA WITH ASIAN SALAD

Tuna is a meaty fish, but do not overcook it because it will become tough. Make sure the pan is hot so you can cook the tuna quickly.

SERVES 2
PREPARATION TIME 15 MINUTES, PLUS MARINATING AND RESTING
COOKING TIME 4–6 MINUTES

2 teaspoons honey
1 teaspoon sesame oil
1½ inch piece of fresh ginger root, grated
2 tuna steaks, about 5 oz each
2–3 tablespoons sesame seeds
juice of 1 lime

FOR THE SALAD
½ cucumber, cut into matchsticks
3 carrots, peeled and cut into matchsticks
6 scallions, shredded
small handful of cilantro leaves

1 Whisk together the honey, oil, and ginger in a small bowl. Put the tuna into a nonmetallic bowl, pour the marinade over it, and let marinate at room temperature for 10 minutes, turning once.

2 Meanwhile, to make the salad, mix together all the ingredients in a bowl. Set aside.

3 Heat a ridged grill pan or a skillet until hot. Spread out the sesame seeds on a plate, then coat the tuna in the seeds.

4 Cook the tuna in the hot pan for 2–3 minutes on each side, or until browned but still pink in the center. Let rest for 2 minutes.

5 Thinly slice the tuna and serve on the salad, drizzled with the lime juice.

CRAB AND AVOCADO SALAD

Creamy avocado, sweet crabmeat, and crunchy pecans make this a delicious Paleo salad.,

SERVES 2
PREPARATION TIME 10 MINUTES, PLUS COOLING
COOKING TIME 3–4 MINUTES

1 tablespoon pecans
2 cups baby spinach leaves
1 cup watercress, mâche, or arugula
1 avocado
4 cherry tomatoes, halved
4 oz white crabmeat

FOR THE DRESSING
2 tablespoons olive oil
juice of 1 lime
½ teaspoon Dijon mustard
½ teaspoon honey
1 tablespoon chopped cilantro

1 Heat a dry, nonstick skillet over medium-low heat and dry-fry the pecans for 3–4 minutes, shaking the pan occasionally, until golden brown and toasted. Set aside.

2 To make the dressing, whisk together all the ingredients in, a small bowl.

3 Divide the spinach leaves and watercress between 2 plates. Halve, pit, and peel the avocado, then slice the flesh and divide between the plates.

4 Top with the remaining ingredients and drizzle with the dressing. Serve immediately.

SHRIMP, WATERMELON, AND AVOCADO SALAD

Enjoy this healthy, tasty salad in the summer. If you have any leftover watermelon, you can put it into a blender and process to make a refreshing smoothie.

SERVES 4
PREPARATION TIME 10 MINUTES, PLUS STANDING

1 small red onion, finely sliced
1 garlic clove, crushed
1 red chile, seeded and finely diced
juice of 1 lime
1 teaspoon honey
2 avocados
¼ watermelon, peeled, seeded, and chopped into bite-size pieces
10 oz cooked, peeled jumbo shrimp
small handful of cilantro leaves, chopped

1 Put the onion, garlic, chile, lime juice, and honey into a large salad bowl and mix together. Let stand for 10 minutes.

2 When ready to serve, halve, pit, and peel the avocados, then chop the flesh and add to the salad bowl with the remaining ingredients. Toss together well and serve immediately.

SHRIMP CAESAR SALAD

This classic recipe is a great lunchtime dish, and you can use shrimp, chicken, turkey, eggs, or even just greens if you are feeling really pure.

SERVES 4
PREPARATION TIME 10 MINUTES

2 romaine lettuce, coarsely torn
8 anchovy fillets
10 oz cooked, peeled jumbo shrimp

FOR THE DRESSING
juice of ½ lemon
1 extra-large egg
1 garlic clove, crushed
2 teaspoons whole-grain mustard
2 anchovy fillets
½ cup extra-virgin olive oil

1 To make the dressing, put the lemon juice, egg, garlic, mustard, and anchovies into a small food processor or blender and blend together. With the motor still running, slowly add the oil through the feeder tube until the dressing starts to thicken.

2 Put the lettuce, anchovies, and shrimp into a serving bowl, then pour the dressing over the salad. Lightly toss together and serve.

FIG AND HAM SALAD

With its mouth-watering combination of sweet figs and slightly salty prosciutto ham, this salad is simple, yet delicious.

SERVES 2
PREPARATION TIME 5 MINUTES

2¼ cups mixed salad greens
8 basil leaves
4 figs, halved
4 slices of prosciutto ham
6 cherry tomatoes, halved
1 tablespoon pecans

FOR THE DRESSING
3 tablespoons olive oil
juice of ½ lemon
½ teaspoon whole-grain mustard
½ teaspoon honey

1 To make the dressing, whisk together all the ingredients in a small bowl.

2 Toss the salad greens and basil together, then divide between 2 plates. Top each one with 2 halved figs and 2 slices of ham.

3 Sprinkle the tomato halves and pecans over the salad, then drizzle with the dressing and serve.

HONEY AND MUSTARD CHICKEN SALAD

This is an easy way to create a deliciously sweet and sticky chicken dish.

SERVES 4
PREPARATION TIME 10 MINUTES
COOKING TIME 10–12 MINUTES

3 boneless, skinless chicken
  breasts, about 5 oz each
2 tablespoons pumpkin seeds
3 cups watercress, mâche,
  or other bitter salad greens
1 cup arugula leaves
1 red bell pepper, cored, seeded,
  and thinly sliced
1 large avocado

FOR THE DRESSING
3 tablespoons olive oil
1 teaspoon honey
1 teaspoon Dijon mustard
1 teaspoon lemon juice

1 To make the dressing, whisk together all the ingredients in a small bowl. Set aside.

2 Cook the chicken breasts under a preheated hot broiler for 5–6 minutes on each side, or until cooked through.

3 Meanwhile, heat a dry, nonstick skillet over medium-low heat and dry-fry the pumpkin seeds for 2–3 minutes, shaking the pan occasionally, until golden and toasted.

4 Toss together the watercress and arugula and place on a serving plate. Sprinkle the sliced red bell pepper over the greens.

5 Halve, pit, and peel the avocado, then slice the flesh. Slice the chicken diagonally and add to the salad greens, then top with the avocado.

6 Sprinkle with the toasted pumpkin seeds and dressing. Serve immediately.

CRISPY DUCK AND CASHEW SALAD

Duck has a lot of fat on it, but if cooked in the right way, it can have crisp skin and tender meat with plenty of flavor.

SERVES 2
PREPARATION TIME 15 MINUTES, PLUS MARINATING
COOKING TIME 7–9 MINUTES

1 teaspoon sesame oil
1 teaspoon honey
1 teaspoon grated fresh ginger root
1 duck breast, about 5 oz, cut into strips
1 tablespoon cashew nuts
juice of ½ lemon
1 bok choy, chopped
1 carrot, peeled and grated
2 scallions, sliced
¼ cucumber, cut into matchsticks
¼ cup bean sprouts

1 Mix together the oil, honey, and ginger in a bowl, then add the duck strips and coat well. Let marinate for 5 minutes.

2 Meanwhile, heat a dry, nonstick skillet over medium-low heat and dry-fry the cashews for 3–4 minutes, shaking the pan occasionally, until golden brown and toasted. Set aside.

3 Heat a skillet or ridged grill pan until hot, add the duck strips, and cook for 4–5 minutes, until crisp and golden.

4 Meanwhile, stir the lemon juice into the remaining marinade to make a dressing.

5 Place the remaining ingredients in a large serving bowl and toss together, then top with the duck. Serve drizzled with the dressing.

SUPERFOOD SALAD

• •

This salad has many wonderful textures and tastes and, on top of all that, it is bursting with goodness.

• •

SERVES 4
PREPARATION TIME 15 MINUTES,
 PLUS COOLING
COOKING TIME 15–18 MINUTES

½ butternut squash, peeled, seeded, and chopped into ½ inch cubes
1 tablespoon olive oil
1 teaspoon cumin seeds
1 head of broccoli, cut into florets
1⅓ cups frozen or fresh peas
¼ cup mixed seeds, such as sunflower, pumpkin, and sesame seeds
1 cup shredded red cabbage
4 tomatoes, chopped
4 cooked beets, cut into wedges
⅔ cup alfalfa sprouts

FOR THE DRESSING
1 tablespoon olive oil
2 tablespoons avocado oil
juice of 1 lemon
½ teaspoon honey
½ teaspoon whole-grain mustard

1 Put the squash into a roasting pan and sprinkle with the olive oil and cumin seeds. Place in a preheated oven, at 400°F, for 15–18 minutes, until tender. Remove from the roasting pan and let cool slightly.

2 Meanwhile, cook the broccoli and peas in a saucepan of boiling water for 4–5 minutes, until tender. Drain, then refresh under cold running water and drain again.

3 Heat a dry, nonstick skillet over medium-low heat and dry-fry the seeds for 2–3 minutes, shaking the pan occasionally, until golden brown and toasted. Let cool.

4 To make the dressing, put all the ingredients into a small bowl and whisk together.

5 Put the cooled squash, drained broccoli and peas, and toasted seeds in a salad bowl, add the remaining ingredients, except the alfalfa sprouts, and toss together with the dressing. Serve the salad topped with the alfalfa sprouts.

ROASTED BEET, WATERCRESS, AND ORANGE SALAD

Beets are great for supporting the detoxification process so, when trying to lose weight, it's good to include it in your diet.

SERVES 4
PREPARATION TIME 15 MINUTES, PLUS COOLING
COOKING TIME 15–20 MINUTES

2 raw beets, peeled and chopped
1½ teaspoons olive oil
½ teaspoon cumin seeds
3 cups watercress, mâche, or other bitter salad greens
2 oranges, pith removed and segmented
1 large carrot, peeled and shredded
¼ cup pecans, coarsely broken

FOR THE DRESSING
2 tablespoons olive oil
1 tablespoon lemon juice
1 teaspoon honey
½ teaspoon whole-grain mustard
½ teaspoon chopped rosemary
freshly ground black pepper

1 Put the beets into a roasting pan and sprinkle with the oil and cumin seeds. Roast in a preheated oven, at 400°F, for 15–20 minutes, until tender. Let cool slightly.

2 To make the dressing, put all the ingredients into a small bowl and whisk together.

3 Put the watercress, orange segments, shredded carrot, and warm roasted beets into a bowl, pour the dressing over the salad, and toss together, then divide among 4 plates. Sprinkle with the pecans and serve.

CRUNCHY INDIAN SALAD

These flavors are typical of Kerala in India, and using ginger and lime brings out the freshness of the mango. You could serve it with freshly cooked shrimp or broiled chicken.

SERVES 2
PREPARATION TIME 10 MINUTES
COOKING TIME 1–2 MINUTES

2 tablespoons sesame seeds
1 red bell pepper, cored, seeded, and finely sliced
3 scallions, shredded
1 ripe mango, peeled, pitted, and cut into matchsticks
1 cup watercress, mâche, or other bitter salad greens

FOR THE DRESSING
¾ inch piece of fresh ginger root, grated
grated zest and juice of 1 lime
1 teaspoon honey
3 tablespoons extra-virgin olive oil
freshly ground black pepper

1 Heat a dry, nonstick skillet over medium-low heat and dry-fry the sesame seeds for 1–2 minutes, shaking the pan occasionally, until golden brown and toasted. Set aside.

2 To make the dressing, put all the ingredients into a small bowl and whisk together.

3 Put the toasted seeds with the remaining ingredients into a large bowl and toss together, then pour the dressing over the salad and toss again before serving.

CHUNKY CUMIN WALDORF SALAD

Waldorf salad has been around since the 1890s and was first created in New York. This Paleo version has made a few simple changes, adding a little spice and omitting the mayonnaise.

SERVES 4
PREPARATION TIME 10 MINUTES
COOKING TIME 3–4 MINUTES

½ cup walnut pieces
⅔ cup halved green grapes
6 celery sticks, sliced diagonally
1 sweet green apple, peeled, cored, and thinly sliced

FOR THE DRESSING
½ cup ground almonds (almond meal)
½ cup nondairy milk
1 teaspoon ground cumin

1 Heat a dry, nonstick skillet over medium-low heat and dry-fry the walnuts for 3–4 minutes, shaking the pan occasionally, until golden brown and toasted. Set aside.

2 To make the dressing, put all the ingredients into a small food processor or blender and blend together.

3 Transfer the dressing to a large bowl, then add the toasted walnuts, grapes, celery, and apple and toss well to coat.

4 Serve immediately, or cover and chill until required.

PALEO TABBOULEH

Who would have thought parsnips could be a good substitute for bulgur wheat? This has a much crunchier texture than traditional tabbouleh, but it is still tasty.

SERVES 4
PREPARATION TIME 10 MINUTES, PLUS STANDING
COOKING TIME 2–3 MINUTES

¼ cup pine nuts
1 parsnip, peeled and
    coarsely chopped
small handful of parsley
small handful of basil leaves
small handful of cilantro leaves
¼ cucumber, diced
juice of ½ lemon
1 tablespoon extra-virgin olive oil
freshly ground black pepper

1 Heat a dry, nonstick skillet over medium-low heat and dry-fry the pine nuts for 2–3 minutes, shaking the pan occasionally, until golden brown and toasted. Set aside.

2 Put the parsnip into a food processor and process until broken down into coarse crumbs. Add the toasted pine nuts and herbs and process again until the mixture resembles bulgur wheat.

3 Transfer the mixture to a bowl, stir in the remaining ingredients, and season with black pepper. Let stand for at least 5 minutes to let the flavors develop.

CRUNCHY KALE SALAD

This flavor-packed salad is great to take to work or on a picnic, because it doesn't wilt.

SERVES 2
PREPARATION TIME 10 MINUTES
COOKING TIME 3–4 MINUTES

½ cup walnut halves
¾ cup thinly shredded kale
1 carrot, peeled and cut into
   thin strips
1 small raw beet, peeled
   and cut into thin strips

FOR THE DRESSING
grated zest and juice of 1 lemon
1 tablespoon extra-virgin olive oil
½ teaspoon sesame oil
freshly ground black pepper

1 Heat a dry, nonstick skillet over medium-low heat and dry-fry the walnuts for 3–4 minutes, shaking the pan occasionally, until golden brown and toasted. Set aside.

2 To make the dressing, whisk together all the ingredients in a small bowl. Put the kale, carrot, and beet into a bowl, pour over the dressing, and toss together.

3 Serve the salad sprinkled with the toasted walnuts.

ORANGE, AVOCADO, AND CASHEW SALAD

This refreshing salad is really quick and easy to make—just the thing when you want to whip up a meal for one.

SERVES 1
PREPARATION TIME 10 MINUTES
COOKING TIME 3–4 MINUTES

2 tablespoons cashews
1 orange
1 avocado
1 cup watercress, mâche,
  or other bitter salad greens
1 tablespoon olive oil

1 Heat a dry, nonstick skillet over medium-low heat and dry-fry the cashews for 3–4 minutes, shaking the pan occasionally, until golden brown and toasted. Set aside.

2 Using a sharp knife, remove the peel and pith from the orange. Hold the orange over a bowl to catch the juice and cut out the segments. Put the orange segments into a separate bowl.

3 Halve, pit, and peel the avocado. Chop the avocado flesh, add to the orange segments, and mix together. Toss the watercress into the bowl.

4 Transfer the salad to a serving plate and sprinkle with the toasted cashews.

5 Add the oil to the reserved orange juice and whisk together. Drizzle the dressing over the salad and serve.

GINGER, SNOW PEA, AND BEAN SPROUT COLESLAW

Not all coleslaw has to be made with cabbage. This tasty version uses other crunchy vegetables, with some spice to liven it up.

SERVES 4
PREPARATION TIME 15 MINUTES,
** PLUS COOLING**
COOKING TIME 3–4 MINUTES

⅓ cup hazelnuts
¾ cup thinly shredded snow peas
1 cup bean sprouts
1 red bell pepper, cored, seeded, and thinly sliced
5 radishes, thinly sliced

FOR THE DRESSING
2 tablespoons olive oil
1 tablespoon lemon juice
1 teaspoon toasted sesame oil
½ lemon grass stalk, outer leaves discarded and finely diced
¾ inch piece of fresh ginger root, peeled and finely diced
1 teaspoon coconut palm sugar (jaggery) or raw sugar

1 Heat a dry, nonstick skillet over medium-low heat and dry-fry the hazelnuts for 3–4 minutes, shaking the pan occasionally, until golden brown and toasted. Let cool slightly, then coarsely chop the nuts and set aside.

2 To make the dressing, put all the ingredients into a small bowl and whisk together until the sugar has dissolved and the dressing has emulsified.

3 Put the toasted nuts and remaining ingredients into a large bowl, pour the dressing over the salad, and toss together to serve.

4

FISH AND SEAFOOD

HONEY AND WASABI-GLAZED SALMON FILLETS

Wasabi is a hot paste that adds plenty of flavor—and heat—to this dish, so use it sparingly.

SERVES 2
PREPARATION TIME 5 MINUTES
COOKING TIME 8 MINUTES

juice of 1 lemon
1 tablespoon honey
1 teaspoon grated fresh ginger root
½–1 teaspoon wasabi paste
1 tablespoon sesame seeds
2 teaspoons coconut oil
2 salmon fillets, about 5 oz each
crisp green salad, to serve

1 Put the lemon juice, honey, ginger, and wasabi paste into a small saucepan and gently heat together. Bring to a simmer, then remove from the heat.

2 Meanwhile, heat a dry, nonstick skillet over medium-low heat and dry-fry the sesame seeds for 1–2 minutes, shaking the pan occasionally, until golden and toasted. Set aside.

3 Heat the oil in a separate skillet or ridged grill pan, add the salmon, skin side up, and cook for 3 minutes. Turn the fish over and cook for another 2 minutes, or until the fish is cooked through.

4 Pour the glaze over the fish, sprinkle with the toasted sesame seeds, and cook for another minute. Serve the salmon with a crisp green salad.

BROILED SALMON WITH AVOCADO SALSA

Both salmon and avocado are rich in essential fats, so it's important that you include them in your diet.

SERVES 2
PREPARATION TIME 10 MINUTES
COOKING TIME 6–8 MINUTES

2 salmon steaks, about 5 oz each
1 cup watercress, arugula leaves, mâche, or other bitter greens

FOR THE SALSA
1 avocado
2 scallions, sliced
10 cherry tomatoes, quartered
1 tablespoon chopped cilantro
juice of ½ lime
½ teaspoon sesame oil

1 To make the salsa, halve, pit, and peel the avocado, then dice the flesh. Put it into a nonmetallic bowl, add the remaining ingredients, and mix together. Let stand.

2 Cook the salmon steaks under a preheated hot broiler for 3–4 minutes on each side, or until the fish is cooked through.

3 Divide the watercress between 2 plates and top with the salmon. Spoon the salsa over the fish and serve.

SALMON AND GRAPEFRUIT CEVICHE

If you love sushi or sashimi, you will enjoy ceviche—the fish is "cooked" by the acidity of the grapefruit juice, which makes it wonderfully tender, too.

SERVES 4
**PREPARATION TIME 10 MINUTES,
   PLUS MARINATING**

1 grapefruit
juice of 1 lime
1 red chile, seeded and
   thinly sliced
4 scallions, sliced
1 tablespoon chopped cilantro
1 lb skinless salmon fillet,
   thinly sliced
crisp salad greens, to serve

1 Cut the grapefruit in half. Squeeze the juice from one of the halves and pour it into a nonmetallic bowl. Using a sharp knife, cut the pith from the remaining half and cut out the segments, then chop and add to the bowl. Stir in the lime juice, chile, scallions, and cilantro.

2 Place the salmon in the marinade and mix well. Cover and let marinate in the refrigerator for 30 minutes.

3 Arrange the salmon slices on a bed of crisp salad greens and serve.

BROILED SALMON WITH COCONUT CABBAGE

If you prefer a spicy version, simply add finely diced red chile to this Indian-inspired recipe.

SERVES 4
PREPARATION TIME 5 MINUTES
COOKING TIME 10–12 MINUTES

1 tablespoon coconut oil
2 teaspoons cumin seeds
1 onion, sliced
½ teaspoon turmeric
½ large savoy cabbage, shredded
1 tablespoon unsweetened
　shredded dried coconut
2 tablespoons water
4 salmon fillets, about 5 oz each
freshly ground black pepper

1 Heat the oil in a large skillet, add the cumin seeds and onion, and cook for 3–4 minutes, until the onion is starting to soften. Stir in the turmeric and cook for another minute.

2 Add the cabbage and coconut and toss to coat with the spices. Add the measured water and bring to a simmer, then cover and cook for 5–6 minutes.

3 Meanwhile, cook the salmon under a preheated hot broiler for 3–4 minutes on each side, or until the fish is cooked through.

4 Uncover the cabbage, toss, and season with black pepper, then serve with the broiled salmon.

THAI SEA BASS PACKAGES

Cooking fish wrapped in baking parchment helps to seal in the flavors and ensure the fish stays moist, too. Ask your fish dealer to scale and gut the fish for you.

SERVES 2
PREPARATION TIME 15 MINUTES
COOKING TIME 20–25 MINUTES

¾ cup peeled and sliced
  fresh ginger root
2 lemon grass stalks, outer leaves
  discarded and sliced
2 garlic cloves, peeled and bruised
1 red chile, seeded and finely diced
grated zest and juice of 1 lime
2 small sea bass, about 1 lb each,
  scaled and gutted
freshly ground black pepper
small handful of cilantro leaves,
  to garnish

1 Mix together the ginger, lemon grass, garlic, chile, and lime zest and juice in a bowl, then fill the cavities of the fish with three-quarters of the mixture.

2 Place each fish on a large piece of baking parchment, sprinkle with the remaining stuffing mixture, and season with black pepper. Fold up the sides of the paper to seal the packages and place them on a baking sheet.

3 Bake in a preheated oven, at 350°F, for 20–25 minutes, until the fish is cooked through and the flesh flakes off the bone.

4 Serve the fish sprinkled with cilantro leaves.

BROILED RED SNAPPER AND ROASTED FENNEL WITH CHILI OIL

Fennel is the perfect accompaniment to fish and, if you can't find red snapper, this recipe works well with sea bream, too.

SERVES 2
PREPARATION TIME 10 MINUTES, PLUS STANDING
COOKING TIME 35 MINUTES

2 fennel bulbs, trimmed and sliced
1 tablespoon olive oil
4 red snapper fillets, about
    5–6 oz each

FOR THE CHILI OIL
2 garlic cloves, finely chopped
1 teaspoon dried red pepper flakes
⅓ cup olive oil
2 tablespoons chopped parsley

1 To make the chili oil, put the garlic, red pepper flakes, and oil into a small saucepan and heat gently for 5 minutes. Remove from the heat and let stand.

2 Put the fennel into a roasting pan and drizzle with the oil. Place in a preheated oven, at 400°F, for 30 minutes, until the fennel is tender.

3 Toward the end of the fennel cooking time, cook the red snapper under a preheated hot broiler for 3–4 minutes on each side, or until the fish is cooked through.

4 Stir the parsley into the chili oil. Spoon the fennel onto 2 warmed plates, top with the fish, and serve drizzled with the chili oil.

PANCETTA-WRAPPED MONKFISH

Monkfish is a solid, meaty fish. Ask your fish dealer to remove the outer membrane of the tail because this can be difficult to do.

SERVES 4
PREPARATION TIME 5 MINUTES, PLUS RESTING
COOKING TIME 16–20 MINUTES

12–14 oz monkfish tail, sliced in half lengthwise
5 oz pancetta slices
1 tablespoon thyme leaves
steamed baby broccoli, to serve

1 Lay the monkfish halves together in opposite directions, so that a thick and a thin end are together at both ends.

2 Lay the pancetta slices on a board, slightly overlapping, then place the monkfish in the center and sprinkle the thyme over it. Wrap the pancetta around the fish to enclose it completely.

3 Cook under a preheated hot broiler for 8–10 minutes on each side, or until the fish is cooked through. Let rest for 2–3 minutes.

4 Slice the fish into medallions and serve with steamed baby broccoli.

PAN-FRIED COD WITH MINTED PEA PUREE

Peas and mint are a great combination. You can serve the pea puree with other fish or seafood. It works particularly well with scallops.

SERVES 2
PREPARATION TIME 10 MINUTES
COOKING TIME 8–11 MINUTES

1 tablespoon olive oil
2 cod fillets, about 5 oz each
1 tablespoon chopped chives, to garnish

FOR THE PUREE
1⅔ cups frozen peas
6–8 mint leaves, chopped
1 tablespoon nondairy milk
freshly ground black pepper

1 To make the puree, cook the peas in a saucepan of boiling water for 2–3 minutes, then drain and place in a food processor or blender with the mint, milk, and some black pepper. Blend until smooth. Alternatively, for a more rustic puree, drain the peas and return to the pan, then mash them with the remaining puree ingredients. Set aside and keep warm.

2 Heat the oil in a skillet, add the cod, and cook for 3–4 minutes on each side, until the fish is cooked through.

3 Divide the pea puree between 2 warmed plates, top with the cod, and serve sprinkled with the chopped chives.

ORANGE AND TOMATO ROASTED COD

Adding orange to this dish gives it a real lift.
For a change of pace, you can use lemon instead.

SERVES 4
PREPARATION TIME 10 MINUTES
COOKING TIME 45–50 MINUTES

8 roma or plum tomatoes, quartered
2 onions, cut into wedges
zest of 1 orange, cut into julienne strips
1 tablespoon thyme leaves
1 tablespoon olive oil
4 cod loins, about 5 oz each
2 tablespoons slivered almonds
freshly ground black pepper
crisp green salad or steamed green vegetables, to serve

1 Put the tomatoes, onions, orange strips, thyme, and oil into a roasting pan, season with black pepper, and mix well. Roast in a preheated oven, at 400°F, for 35–40 minutes, stirring once, until the onions start to caramelize.

2 Increase the oven temperature to 425°F. Remove the pan from the oven, nestle the cod loins in the vegetables, spooning some over the fish. Sprinkle with the slivered almonds.

3 Return to the oven and roast for 10–12 minutes, until the cod is cooked through. Serve with a crisp green salad or steamed greens.

BROILED COD WITH PESTO AND GREEN BEANS

Store-bought pesto includes Parmesan, which is not allowed on the Paleo diet. The pesto in this recipe is just as delicious, and you could make a bigger batch of it and store in the refrigerator for a few days.

SERVES 2
PREPARATION TIME 10 MINUTES, PLUS COOLING
COOKING TIME 8–11 MINUTES

2 cod loins, about 5 oz each
1½ cups trimmed green beans

FOR THE PESTO
2 tablespoons pine nuts
large handful of basil leaves
1 small garlic clove, chopped
3–4 tablespoons olive oil

1 To make the pesto, heat a dry, nonstick skillet over medium-low heat and dry-fry the pine nuts for 2–3 minutes, shaking the pan occasionally, until golden brown and toasted. Let cool.

2 Put the basil, toasted pine nuts, and garlic into a small food processor or blender and process until broken down. With the motor still running, slowly add the oil through the feeder tube until it forms a loose paste. Set aside.

3 Cook the cod under a preheated hot broiler for 3–4 minutes on each side, or until the fish is cooked through.

4 Meanwhile, put the green beans in a steamer, cover, and cook for 3–4 minutes, until just tender.

5 Toss the green beans in the pesto, then divide between 2 warmed plates. Top with the broiled cod and serve.

BROILED COD WITH PEPERONATA

Peperonata is a traditional Italian dish of sweet bell peppers and onions that can be served on its own or to accompany broiled fish.

SERVES 4
PREPARATION TIME 15 MINUTES
COOKING TIME 45 MINUTES

4 ripe tomatoes (about 1 lb)
¼ cup olive oil
2 onions, chopped
2 garlic cloves, crushed
4 red bell peppers, cored, seeded, and thickly sliced
2 yellow bell peppers, cored, seeded, and thickly sliced
6–8 basil leaves, coarsely torn
4 cod loins, about 5 oz each
freshly ground black pepper

1 Put the tomatoes into a heatproof bowl and pour over enough boiling water to cover. Let stand for 1–2 minutes, then drain, cut a cross at the stem end of each tomato, and peel off the skins. Chop the flesh and set aside.

2 Heat the oil in a large skillet, add the onions and garlic, and cook for 4–5 minutes, stirring occasionally, until softened. Add the bell peppers and cook over medium heat for another 12 minutes.

3 Stir in the tomatoes and basil, season with black pepper, and continue to cook for 30 minutes, stirring occasionally.

4 Toward the end of the peperonata cooking time, cook the cod under a preheated hot broiler for 3–4 minutes on each side, or until the fish is cooked through. Serve the cod on the peperonata.

MUSHROOM-STUFFED TROUT

This looks impressive, but it is actually simple to make and tastes delicious.

SERVES 4
PREPARATION TIME 15 MINUTES
COOKING TIME 35–40 MINUTES

2 tablespoons olive oil
1 onion, finely chopped
1 garlic clove, crushed
5 cups chopped cremini
    mushrooms
1½ cups slivered almonds
2 tablespoons chopped cilantro
2 whole trout, about 1½–1¾ lb
    each, cleaned and gutted
freshly ground black pepper
steamed broccoli, to serve

1 Heat the oil in a skillet, add the onion, and cook for 4–5 minutes, until softened. Add the garlic and mushrooms and cook for another 6–8 minutes, until the mushrooms are tender. Remove from the heat, add the slivered almonds and cilantro, and mix well.

2 Season the fish with black pepper inside and out, then stuff with the mushroom filling. Wrap each one loosely in aluminum foil and place on a baking sheet.

3 Bake in a preheated oven, at 400°F, for 25 minutes, or until the fish is just cooked through. Serve with steamed broccoli.

MACKEREL CURRY

Mackerel is one of the oily fish that are rich in omega-3 essential fats—vital for a healthy diet.

SERVES 4
PREPARATION TIME 10 MINUTES
COOKING TIME 16–20 MINUTES

1 tablespoon coconut oil
1 teaspoon cumin seeds
1 large onion, sliced
⅔ cup coconut milk
1 cup water
1 lb fresh mackerel fillets, skinned
   and cut into 2 inch pieces
small handful of cilantro leaves,
   coarsely torn
freshly ground black pepper

FOR THE CURRY PASTE
1 green chile, seeded and chopped
1 teaspoon ground coriander
½ teaspoon turmeric
4 garlic cloves
1 inch piece of fresh ginger root,
   peeled and chopped
1 teaspoon coconut oil

TO SERVE
wilted spinach leaves
lemon wedges

1 To make the curry paste, put all the ingredients into a small food processor or blender and blend until smooth.

2 Heat the oil in a wok or skillet, add the paste and the cumin seeds, and cook for 2–3 minutes. Add the onion and cook for another 1–2 minutes, until starting to soften.

3 Pour in the coconut milk and measured water and bring to a boil, then reduce the heat and simmer for 5 minutes. Season with black pepper.

4 Add the mackerel to the pan and cook for 6–8 minutes, until the fish is cooked through. Stir in the cilantro leaves.

5 Serve the curry with wilted spinach and lemon wedges.

GINGER AND ORANGE MACKEREL WITH COLESLAW

Here, coleslaw gets its creaminess from a delicious cashew nut dressing.

SERVES 4
**PREPARATION TIME 20 MINUTES,
  PLUS MARINATING**
COOKING TIME 25–30 MINUTES

4 fresh mackerel fillets,
  about 5 oz each
juice of 2 oranges
grated zest of 1 orange
1 teaspoon grated fresh
  ginger root
2 teaspoons tomato paste

FOR THE COLESLAW
½ cup cashew nuts
2 scallions, chopped
juice of ½ lemon
½ teaspoon honey
¼ red cabbage, shredded
¼ green cabbage, shredded
2 carrots, peeled and shredded
small handful of cilantro leaves

1 Put the mackerel fillets into a nonmetallic ovenproof dish. Mix together the orange juice, orange zest, ginger, and tomato paste in a small bowl, then pour the marinade over the mackerel. Cover and let marinate in the refrigerator for at least 30 minutes.

2 To make the dressing for the coleslaw, put the cashew nuts, scallions, lemon juice, and honey into a food processor or blender and blend until smooth, gradually adding enough water to form the consistency of thick heavy cream.

3 Mix together the cabbages, carrots, and cilantro in a large bowl, then pour the dressing over the vegetables and toss together. Let stand.

4 Cover the mackerel in the dish with aluminum foil and bake in a preheated oven, at 400°F, for 25–30 minutes, until the fish is cooked through. Serve with the coleslaw.

MACKEREL FILLETS WITH FENNEL COLESLAW

Mackerel is quick to cook in a skillet or ridged grill pan and also great cooked over grill for a barbecue.

SERVES 4
PREPARATION TIME 15 MINUTES
COOKING TIME 4–6 MINUTES

1 tablespoon olive oil
4 fresh mackerel fillets,
    about 5 oz each

FOR THE COLESLAW
2 tablespoons olive oil
juice of ½ lemon
1 teaspoon honey
½ teaspoon whole-grain mustard
¼ cup chopped dill
2 celery sticks, thinly sliced
½ cucumber, thinly sliced
1 fennel bulb, trimmed and
    thinly sliced
freshly ground black pepper
    (optional)

1 To make the dressing for the coleslaw, whisk together the oil, lemon juice, honey, mustard, and dill in a small bowl. Season with black pepper, if desired.

2 Mix together the celery, cucumber, and fennel in a large bowl, then pour the dressing over the vegetables and toss together. Let stand.

3 Heat the oil in a skillet or ridged grill pan, add the mackerel, and cook for 2–3 minutes on each side, or until the fish is cooked through. Alternatively, cook the fish on a grill.

4 Divide the coleslaw among 4 plates, top with the mackerel, and serve.

LEMON AND PARSLEY SARDINES

Containing omega-3 essential fats and calcium, sardines are cheap and good for you. And if it's a sunny day, you can cook barbecue them.

SERVES 4
PREPARATION TIME 10 MINUTES
COOKING TIME 6–8 MINUTES

4–8 sardines, depending
   on their size
2 lemons
1 tablespoon olive oil
¼ cup slivered almonds
freshly ground black pepper
1 tablespoon chopped parsley,
   to garnish

1 Wash the sardines to remove all the scales, then slash each side a couple of times, using a sharp knife.

2 Squeeze the juice from 1 of the lemons, then rub it all over the sardines, especially into the cuts, with the black pepper.

3 Heat the oil in a skillet or ridged grill pan. Cut the remaining lemon into wedges and add to the pan. Add the sardines and cook for 3–4 minutes on each side, or until the fish is cooked through.

4 Meanwhile, heat a dry, nonstick skillet over medium-low heat and dry-fry the slivered almonds for 2–3 minutes, shaking the pan occasionally, until golden brown and toasted.

5 Serve the sardines sprinkled with the toasted almonds and the parsley.

TUNA CARPACCIO

Ask your fish dealer for the freshest fish he has, from a sustainable source, for this raw fish recipe.

SERVES 4
PREPARATION TIME 15 MINUTES

1 lb fresh tuna
4 radishes, thinly sliced
¼ cucumber, thinly sliced
4 scallions, thinly sliced
juice of 1 lime
1 tablespoon extra-virgin olive oil
freshly ground black pepper

1 Using a sharp knife, cut the tuna into particuarly thin strips, then place on a large serving plate.

2 Sprinkle the radishes, cucumber, and scallions around the plate, then sprinkle with the lime juice, olive oil, and black pepper. Serve immediately.

FISH TAGINE

This is a fragrant fish dish based on the spices used in Morocco. Try it with halibut, cod, or any white fish of your choice.

SERVES 4
PREPARATION TIME 15 MINUTES, PLUS MARINATING
COOKING TIME 25–30 MINUTES

4 halibut or cod fillets, about
    5 oz each
1 tablespoon olive oil
1 large onion, sliced
2 garlic cloves, coarsely chopped
1 teaspoon ground cumin
1 teaspoon paprika
1 (14½ oz) can diced tomatoes
1¼ cups fish stock
grated zest of 1 lemon
2 red bell peppers, cored,
    seeded, and chopped
½ small bunch of cilantro, chopped
juice of ½ lemon

FOR THE MARINADE
1 tablespoon olive oil
2 garlic cloves, coarsely chopped
1 teaspoon ground cumin
1 teaspoon paprika
½ small bunch of cilantro
juice of ½ lemon

1 To make the marinade, put all the ingredients into a small food processor or blender and blend until smooth. Place the fish in a nonmetallic dish and spoon the marinade over it. Cover and let marinate in the refrigerator.

2 Meanwhile, heat the oil in a large saucepan, add the onion and garlic, and cook for 4–5 minutes, until softened. Stir in the cumin and paprika and cook for another 2 minutes.

3 Stir in the tomatoes, stock, and lemon zest and simmer for 8–10 minutes. Add the bell peppers, cover, and continue to cook for 5–6 minutes, until the bell peppers start to soften.

4 Stir in the chopped cilantro, then place the fish on top, cover, and cook for 4–6 minutes, or until the fish is cooked through. Serve drizzled with the lemon juice.

FISH STEW

You can use any meaty fish for this stew—
pollock, cod, tilapia, or even salmon all work well.

SERVES 4
PREPARATION TIME 10 MINUTES
COOKING TIME 16–20 MINUTES

1 tablespoon olive oil
1 onion, chopped
2 garlic cloves, crushed
1 teaspoon ground cumin
½ teaspoon paprika
1 (14½ oz) can diced tomatoes
1 cup fish stock
1 red bell pepper, cored,
    seeded, and chopped
1 lb skinless fish fillets,
    cut into large chunks
4 oz cooked, peeled jumbo shrimp
small handful of cilantro leaves
lemon wedges, to serve

1 Heat the oil in a large saucepan, add the onion, garlic, cumin, and paprika, and cook for 3–4 minutes, until the onion is softened.

2 Add the tomatoes, stock, and red bell pepper and bring to a simmer, then cook for 8–10 minutes.

3 Add the fish and shrimp to the tomato mixture and cook for another 4–5 minutes, until the fish is cooked through.

4 Stir in the cilantro and serve with lemon wedges.

SQUID WITH TOMATOES

Squid is now easier to find, but ask your fish dealer to prepare it for you because it has a tough outer skin that needs to be removed.

SERVES 4
PREPARATION TIME 10 MINUTES
COOKING TIME 20–25 MINUTES

1 tablespoon olive oil
1 red onion, diced
2 garlic cloves, chopped
1 red chile, seeded and finely diced
pinch of paprika
1 (14½ oz) can diced tomatoes
1 lb fresh squid, prepared and
　　cut into rings
grated rind of 1 lemon
small handful of parsley leaves
freshly ground black pepper

1 Heat the oil in a skillet, add the onion, garlic, and chile, and cook for 2–3 minutes, until starting to soften.

2 Stir in the paprika, then pour in the tomatoes. Bring to a boil, then reduce the heat and simmer for 12–15 minutes.

3 Add the squid to the pan, cover, and cook for 5 minutes until the squid is tender and cooked through.

4 Stir in the lemon zest and parsley, season with black pepper, and serve.

MUSSELS IN SPICY TOMATOES

Mussels are cheap, sustainable, and delightfully simple to cook.

SERVES 2
PREPARATION TIME 20 MINUTES
COOKING TIME 7–10 MINUTES

2 tomatoes
2 tablespoons olive oil
2 garlic cloves, chopped
1 shallot, diced
1 red chile, seeded and
    finely diced
1 cup water
1 teaspoon tomato paste
2 lb mussels, scrubbed and
    debearded (discard any
    with broken shells or that
    don't close when tapped)
freshly ground black pepper
handful of basil leaves, coarsely
    torn, to garnish

1 Put the tomatoes into a heatproof bowl and pour over enough boiling water to cover. Let stand for 1–2 minutes, then drain, cut a cross at the stem end of each tomato, and peel off the skins. Halve and seed, then coarsely chop the flesh.

2 Heat the oil in a large saucepan that has a tight-fitting lid, add the garlic, shallot, and chile, and cook for 2–3 minutes, until starting to soften. Stir in the measured water and tomato paste, then season with black pepper. Simmer for 1–2 minutes.

3 Add the mussels and stir. Cover the pan tightly and let cook for 3–4 minutes, shaking the pan a couple of times, until all the shells have opened. Discard any mussels that remain shut.

4 Divide between 2 warmed bowls and serve sprinkled with the basil.

CRAB AND SWEET POTATO CAKES

These are delicious and can be made in advance and chilled until you want to cook them. They are perfect as a packed lunch or to take on a picnic.

SERVES 4
PREPARATION TIME 20 MINUTES, PLUS COOLING
COOKING TIME 20–30 MINUTES

2 sweet potatoes, peeled and chopped
1 tablespoon olive oil
12 oz crabmeat, a mixture of dark and white meat
¼ red bell pepper, cored, seeded, and finely diced
2 tablespoons chopped chives
2 tablespoons coconut flour or almond flour
1 tablespoon coconut oil
freshly ground black pepper

1 Put the sweet potatoes into a roasting pan and toss with the olive oil, then roast in a preheated oven, at 400°F, for 15–20 minutes, until tender. Transfer to a bowl and coarsely mash, then let cool for 5–6 minutes.

2 Add the crabmeat, red bell pepper, and chives, season with black pepper, and mix together until well combined. Using wet hands, shape the mixture into 8 small cakes.

3 Put the coconut flour in a small bowl, then toss the potato cakes in the flour to coat.

4 Heat the coconut oil in a large skillet, add the cakes, and cook for 3–4 minutes on each side, until golden. Serve hot or cold.

SPICY SEARED SCALLOPS WITH MANGO AND AVOCADO SALSA

If you like scallops, you will love this recipe, where they are served with a fruity salsa on the side.

SERVES 2
PREPARATION TIME 10 MINUTES
COOKING TIME 4–6 MINUTES

6 scallops
½ tablespoon mild curry powder
1 tablespoon olive oil

FOR THE SALSA
1 small avocado
1 small mango, peeled, pitted,
    and diced
¼ cucumber, diced
juice of ½ lime
1 tablespoon olive oil

1 To make the salsa, halve, pit, and peel the avocado, then dice the flesh and put it into a nonmetallic bowl. Stir in the mango and cucumber, then drizzle with the lime juice and oil. Let stand.

2 Sprinkle the scallops with the curry powder. Heat the oil in a skillet, add the scallops, and cook over high heat for 2–3 minutes on each side, until just golden.

3 Divide the scallops between 2 plates and serve with spoonfuls of the salsa.

SEAFOOD STIR-FRY

If your fish dealer sells mixed seafood, you can just replace the shrimp, squid, and mussels with 1 lb of mixed seafood.

SERVES 4
PREPARATION TIME 10 MINUTES,
  PLUS MARINATING
COOKING TIME 7–10 MINUTES

2 teaspoons honey
grated zest and juice of 1 lime
24 raw, peeled jumbo shrimp
  (about 8oz)
3 oz cooked squid rings
4 oz cooked, shelled mussels
1 tablespoon coconut oil
1 teaspoon sesame oil
4 scallions, sliced
1 red bell pepper, cored, seeded,
  and sliced
1 yellow bell pepper, cored,
  seeded, and sliced
1½ cups bean sprouts
2 cups chopped bok choy

1 Mix together the honey, lime zest, and juice in a small bowl. Put the shrimp, squid, and mussels into a nonmetallic bowl and pour the marinade over the seafood. Let marinate for 5 minutes.

2 Heat the oils in a wok, add the drained seafood, and stir-fry for 2–3 minutes, until the shrimp turn pink. Remove from the pan and set aside.

3 Add the scallions and bell peppers to the pan and stir-fry for 2 minutes, then add the bean sprouts and bok choy and stir-fry for another 1–2 minutes.

4 Return the seafood to the pan and stir-fry for 2–3 minutes, until piping hot. Serve immediately.

THAI GREEN SHRIMP CURRY

Preparing your own Thai curry paste is easy. It tastes much better than store-bought and you can make it as hot as you desire. The paste can be kept in the refrigerator for up to a week.

SERVES 4
PREPARATION TIME 15 MINUTES, PLUS COOLING
COOKING TIME 25–30 MINUTES

1 tablespoon coconut oil
1 eggplant, chopped
1⅔ cups coconut milk
1½ cups snow peas
½ cup fish stock
1 lb raw, peeled jumbo shrimp
grated zest and juice of 1 lime
2 tablespoons chopped cilantro

FOR THE CURRY PASTE
1 teaspoon coriander seeds
1 teaspoon cumin seeds
4 fresh green Thai chiles, chopped
1 inch piece of fresh ginger root, peeled and chopped
4 garlic cloves, chopped
1 shallot, finely chopped
1 lemon grass stalk, outer leaves discarded and finely chopped
1 small bunch of cilantro, including the stems
2 kaffir lime leaves
1 tablespoon Thai fish sauce

1 Heat a dry, nonstick skillet over medium-low heat and dry-fry the coriander seeds and cumin seeds for 3–4 minutes, until lightly toasted and fragrant. Let cool.

2 To make the curry paste, put the toasted seeds and the remaining ingredients into a food processor or blender and blend until nearly smooth. Transfer to an airtight container and store for up to 1 week in the refrigerator.

3 Heat the oil in a large skillet or wok, add the eggplant, and cook for 10–12 minutes, until golden brown and softened. Stir in 2 tablespoons of the curry paste and cook for another 3–4 minutes.

4 Pour in the coconut milk and bring to a boil, then reduce the heat to a simmer, add the snow peas, and cook for a few minutes. Then add the stock and shrimp and cook for 4–5 minutes, until the shrimp turn pink and are cooked through.

5 Stir in the lime zest and juice and chopped cilantro, then ladle into 4 warmed bowls and serve.

SHRIMP AND EGG STIR-FRY

Everyone loves a stir-fry—it's quick to make and only one pan to wash.

SERVES 2
PREPARATION TIME 5 MINUTES
COOKING TIME 10 MINUTES

1 tablespoon coconut oil
4 oz cooked, peeled shrimp
¾ inch piece of fresh ginger root, grated
1 garlic clove, crushed
½ cup bean sprouts
4 scallions, sliced
1 bok choy, chopped
4 eggs, beaten
small handful of cilantro leaves, coarsely torn

1 Heat the oil in a wok or large skillet, add the shrimp, and stir-fry for 30 seconds, then add the ginger, garlic, bean sprouts, half the scallions, and the bok choy and stir-fry for another minute.

2 Reduce the temperature and add the eggs, leaving them to set a little before moving them around with a spatula or chopsticks until scrambled.

3 Stir in the remaining scallions and the cilantro and serve.

5

MEAT, POULTRY, AND GAME

MOROCCAN BEEF KEBABS

Choose good-quality meat for this dish and, for a wonderful flavor, cook the kebabs over a barbecue grill.

SERVES 4
PREPARATION TIME 15 MINUTES, PLUS MARINATING
COOKING TIME 6–8 MINUTES

2 tablespoons olive oil
juice of 1 lemon
2 garlic cloves, crushed
2 tablespoons chopped cilantro
2 teaspoons ground coriander
2 teaspoons ground cumin
½ teaspoon dried red pepper flakes
¼ teaspoon ground cinnamon
1½ lb lean steak, cut into bite-size pieces
crisp green salad, to serve

1 Mix together the oil, lemon juice, garlic, chopped cilantro, and spices in a nonmetallic bowl. Add the pieces of beef and toss well to coat in the spicy oil. Cover and let marinate in the refrigerator for 1 hour.

2 Thread the beef onto 8 metal skewers, then cook under a preheated hot broiler or on a barbecue grill for 3–4 minutes on each side, or until browned and cooked to your preference.

3 Serve with a crisp green salad.

SPICY BEEF STIR-FRY

Use lean steak for this spicy stir-fry, and vary the vegetables depending on what's in season. If you want some heat, add a diced red chile to the pan with the garlic.

SERVES 2
PREPARATION TIME 10 MINUTES
COOKING TIME 8–9 MINUTES

1 tablespoon coconut oil
8 oz lean beef steak, cut into thin strips
2 teaspoons Chinese five-spice powder
1 garlic clove, crushed
1 inch piece of fresh ginger root, peeled and finely diced
4 scallions, sliced
4 cups shredded collard greens
2 tablespoons water

1 Heat the oil in a wok or large skillet, add the beef, and stir-fry for 2–3 minutes, until starting to brown.

2 Add the five-spice powder, garlic, and ginger and stir-fry for another minute, then stir in the scallions and collard greens.

3 Add the measured water and stir-fry until the greens have wilted. Serve immediately.

TENDERLOIN STEAK WITH SWEET POTATO FRIES

This simple dinner recipe for two can be served with a fresh green salad if you want to add some color to your plate.

SERVES 2
PREPARATION TIME 5 MINUTES, PLUS RESTING
COOKING TIME 18–20 MINUTES

2 sweet potatoes, scrubbed, peeled, and cut into thin strips
1 tablespoon olive oil
2 lean tenderloin steaks, about 5 oz each
freshly ground black pepper

1 Put the sweet potatoes into a large roasting pan. Drizzle with the oil, then sprinkle with black pepper and toss well.

2 Spread the strips out in an even layer and place in a preheated oven, at 400°F, for 18–20 minutes, until tender and golden.

3 Meanwhile, heat a ridged grill pan until hot, add the steak, and cook to your preference. Let rest for 5 minutes. Serve with the fries.

STEAK WITH MUSHROOM AND RED WINE SAUCE

Choose your favorite cut of meat for this dish—keep it lean and organic, if possible, and always let rest before serving, to retain the tenderness of the steak.

SERVES 1
PREPARATION TIME 5 MINUTES, PLUS RESTING
COOKING TIME 12–15 MINUTES

1 tablespoon olive oil
2 shallots, diced
1 cup sliced cremini mushrooms
½ cup red wine
1 lean steak, about 6 oz
crisp green salad, to serve

1 Heat the oil in a skillet, add the shallots, and cook for 3–4 minutes, until softened. Add the mushrooms and cook for another 4–5 minutes, until tender. Pour in the wine, then bring to a boil and reduce by half.

2 Meanwhile, heat a ridged grill pan or preheat the broiler until hot, then cook the steak to your preference. Let rest for 5 minutes.

3 Spoon the mushroom sauce over the steak and serve with a crisp green salad.

GRILLED LIVER WITH MASHED SWEET POTATOES

Overcooked liver can be tough, so make sure the grill pan is hot and cook the liver quickly.

SERVES 4
PREPARATION TIME 15 MINUTES
COOKING TIME 30–35 MINUTES

1 teaspoon cumin seeds
3 tablespoons olive oil
2 large onions, sliced
2 thyme sprigs
8 carrots (about 1 lb),
    peeled and chopped
3 sweet potatoes (about 1 lb),
    peeled and chopped
1 lb liver, sliced
freshly ground black pepper

1 Heat a small, dry nonstick skillet over medium-low heat and dry-fry the cumin seeds for 2–3 minutes, until golden brown and toasted. Set aside.

2 Heat 2 tablespoons of the oil in a separate skillet, add the onions and thyme, and cook over low heat for about 30 minutes, stirring occasionally, until the onions start to caramelize.

3 Meanwhile, cook the carrots and sweet potatoes in a large saucepan of simmering water for 12–15 minutes, until tender.

4 Toward the end of the cooking time, heat a ridged grill pan until hot and drizzle with the remaining oil. Cook the liver for 2–3 minutes on each side, depending on its thickness and until cooked to your preference.

5 Drain the carrots and potatoes, then return to the pan, add the toasted cumin seeds, and mash together. Season the onions with black pepper.

6 Serve the liver on the mashed potatoes, topped with the onions.

MOROCCAN RACK OF LAMB

This is somewhat of a spicy dish; if you want to make it milder, just use less chili powder. Be sure to ask your butcher to trim the excess fat off the rack of lamb.

SERVES 2
PREPARATION TIME 10 MINUTES,
  PLUS RESTING
COOKING TIME 15–25 MINUTES

2 tablespoons olive oil
½ teaspoon ground cumin
½ teaspoon chili powder
¼ teaspoon turmeric
¼ teaspoon paprika
¼ teaspoon ground coriander
2 garlic cloves, crushed
3 tablespoons chopped parsley
juice of ½ lemon
6-cutlet rack of lamb
steamed kale, to serve

1 Mix together the oil, all the spices, garlic, parsley, and lemon juice in a bowl. Put the rack of lamb into a roasting pan and spread the spice mixture over the top.

2 Roast in a preheated oven, at 400°F, for 15–25 minutes, depending on how rare you prefer your lamb. Let rest for 5–6 minutes.

3 Serve with steamed kale.

LAMB AND ROSEMARY STEW

When cutting the lamb into cubes, try to trim off as much fat as you can to make this stew as healthy as possible.

SERVES 4
PREPARATION TIME 15 MINUTES
COOKING TIME 40 MINUTES

1 tablespoon olive oil
1 lb shoulder of lamb, cut into small cubes
1 onion, chopped
2 carrots, peeled and diced
2 garlic cloves, chopped
1½ teaspoons chopped rosemary leaves
1 cup chicken stock
1 (14½ oz) can diced tomatoes
grated zest and juice of 1 lemon
2 tablespoons chopped parsley

1 Heat the oil in a skillet, add the meat, in batches if necessary, and cook until browned all over.

2 Add the onion and cook, stirring, for 3–4 minutes, until starting to soften, then stir in the carrots, garlic, and rosemary and cook for another 3–4 minutes.

3 Pour in the stock and tomatoes, bring to a boil, then reduce the heat and simmer for 20 minutes.

4 Stir in the lemon zest and juice and chopped parsley and cook for another minute before serving.

MUSHROOM AND SPINACH-STUFFED PORK TENDERLOIN

This impressive-looking dish is the perfect choice when you have friends coming to dinner.

SERVES 4
PREPARATION TIME 15 MINUTES, PLUS RESTING
COOKING TIME 55 MINUTES

1 tablespoon olive oil
2 bacon slices, chopped
½ small onion, diced
1 garlic clove, finely chopped
2 cups chopped cremini mushrooms
1½ teaspoons chopped thyme
1½ teaspoons chopped rosemary
5 cups baby spinach leaves
1–1¼ lb pork tenderloin
steamed vegetables, to serve

1 Heat the oil in a skillet, add the bacon, and cook for 3–4 minutes, until cooked through. Remove with a slotted spoon and set aside.

2 Add the onion and garlic to the pan and cook for 2–3 minutes, until starting to soften. Add the mushrooms and herbs and cook for another 3–4 minutes, until the mushrooms are tender.

3 Stir in the spinach and toss until starting to wilt. Remove the pan from the heat and stir in the reserved bacon.

4 Cut down the middle of the tenderloin to open it like a book. Spread the stuffing mixture over the meat, then roll it up to enclose the filling. Secure with toothpicks at the ends.

5 Place the stuffed tenderloin in a roasting pan and bake in a preheated oven, at 375°F, for 45 minutes, until cooked through. Let rest for 10 minutes.

6 Slice the pork and serve with steamed vegetables.

BAKED PORK CHOPS WITH FENNEL AND BUTTERNUT SQUASH

A comforting and satisfying dish, this winter warmer can be cooked in one dish.

SERVES 4
PREPARATION TIME 15 MINUTES
COOKING TIME 45–50 MINUTES

2 tablespoons fennel seeds
1 tablespoon olive oil
4 pork chops or cutlets, fat trimmed
1 large onion, sliced
2 garlic cloves, sliced
½ butternut squash, seeded and cut into bite-size pieces, skin on
2 fennel bulbs, trimmed and sliced
juice of 1 lemon
¼ cup water

1 Crush the fennel seeds in a mortar and pestle and mix with half the oil. Rub the mixture over the pork chops and set aside.

2 Heat the remaining oil in a Dutch oven or flameproof casserole, add the onion and garlic, and cook for 3–4 minutes, until starting to soften, then add the squash and cook for another 3–4 minutes.

3 Stir in the fennel, lemon juice, and measured water, cover with a lid, and transfer to a preheated oven, at 400°F, for 25 minutes.

4 Remove the lid and stir gently, then place the pork chops on top. Return to the oven, uncovered, and cook for another 12–15 minutes, until the pork is tender and cooked through.

PORK, APPLE, AND SAGE BURGERS WITH HONEYED ONIONS

Everyone loves a burger, and these are bursting with the flavor of fresh sage and apples.

SERVES 4
PREPARATION TIME 10 MINUTES,
   PLUS CHILLING
COOKING TIME 35 MINUTES

2 tablespoons olive oil
3 red onions, sliced
1 tablespoon honey
1¾ lb ground pork
3 shallots, finely chopped
1 Granny Smith or other cooking
   apple, peeled and grated
1 egg, beaten
2 tablespoons chopped sage
freshly ground black pepper

1 Heat 1 tablespoon of the oil in a skillet, add the onions, and cook for 5 minutes, until starting to soften, then drizzle with the honey and season with black pepper. Reduce the heat to low and cook for 30 minutes, stirring occasionally.

2 Meanwhile, mix together the pork, shallots, apple, egg, and sage in a large bowl, then shape into 4 burgers. Chill for 10 minutes.

3 Heat the remaining oil in a separate skillet, add the burgers, and cook for 5–6 minutes on each side, or until cooked through. Serve topped with the honeyed onions.

LEMON PORK AND MIXED PEPPER KEBABS

Ideal for a barbecue, these delicious kebabs use lean pork tenderloin.

SERVES 4
PREPARATION TIME 15 MINUTES, PLUS MARINATING
COOKING TIME 12–15 MINUTES

2 tablespoons chopped rosemary
2 tablespoons olive oil
1 garlic clove, chopped
juice of 1 lemon
1¼ lb pork tenderloin, cut into bite-size pieces
2 red bell peppers, cored, seeded, and chopped
1 yellow bell pepper, cored, seeded, and chopped
freshly ground black pepper
lemon wedges, to serve

1 Mix together the rosemary, oil, garlic, and lemon juice in a nonmetallic bowl and season with black pepper. Add the pork and mix to coat well. Let marinate for 15 minutes.

2 Thread the pork and mixed bell peppers alternately onto 8 metal skewers.

3 Cook on a barbecue grill or under a preheated hot broiler for 12–15 minutes, turning and basting with the marinade occasionally, until the pork is cooked through and the bell peppers are tender. Serve with lemon wedges.

BROILED PANCETTA-WRAPPED RADICCHIO

Broiling radicchio may seem strange, but it brings out the sweetness and creates a tasty texture.

SERVES 4
PREPARATION TIME 5 MINUTES, PLUS STANDING
COOKING TIME 5–6 MINUTES

2 tablespoons olive oil
juice of ½ lemon
3 garlic cloves, crushed
1 tablespoon chopped rosemary
4 heads of radicchio, cut into quarters through the core end
8 slices of pancetta, halved lengthwise
freshly ground black pepper

1 Whisk together the oil, lemon juice, garlic, and rosemary in a large bowl and season with black pepper. Add the radicchio and toss to coat, then let stand for 10 minutes.

2 Wrap each radicchio quarter in a halved slice of pancetta. Cook under a preheated hot broiler or on a barbecue grill for 5–6 minutes, turning occasionally, until the edges are crisp and slightly charred. Serve drizzled with the remaining marinade.

SUMMER VEGGIE AND EGGS WITH CRISPY BACON

You can use any variety of vegetables for this dish—even leftover vegetables work well.

SERVES 2
PREPARATION TIME 5 MINUTES
COOKING TIME 11–14 MINUTES

1 tablespoon olive oil
2 bacon slices, chopped
2 zucchini, coarsely chopped
12 cherry tomatoes, halved
1 cup snow peas
3–4 basil leaves, coarsely torn
2 extra-large eggs

1 Heat the oil in a skillet, add the bacon, and cook until crisp. Remove from the pan with a slotted spoon and set aside.

2 Add the zucchini to the pan and cook for 5–6 minutes, stirring occasionally, until starting to soften. Add the tomatoes, snow peas, and basil and cook for another 1–2 minutes.

3 Make 2 hollows in the mixture and crack an egg into each hollow. Cover the pan with a lid or aluminum foil and cook for 2–3 minutes, or until the egg whites are set and the eggs are cooked to your preference. Serve sprinkled with the crispy bacon.

CHICKEN PACKAGES WITH ROASTED RATATOUILLE

Succulent chicken and roasted vegetables combine in this mouth-watering recipe.

SERVES 4
PREPARATION TIME 15 MINUTES
COOKING TIME 25–30 MINUTES

1 eggplant, cut into cubes
1 red bell pepper, cored, seeded, and chopped
1 yellow bell pepper, cored, seeded, and chopped
1 red onion, cut into wedges
2 zucchini, sliced
¼ cup olive oil
4 boneless, skinless chicken breasts, about 5 oz each
8 tarragon sprigs
½ cup water
freshly ground black pepper

1 Put the vegetables into a roasting pan and toss with 2 tablespoons of the oil. Roast in a preheated oven, at 400°F, for 25–30 minutes, until just starting to char at the edges.

2 Meanwhile, put each chicken breast onto a large piece of baking parchment. Add 2 sprigs of tarragon to each, then sprinkle each one with 2 tablespoons of the measured water and season with black pepper. Fold up the sides of the paper to seal the packages and place them on a baking sheet or in a roasting pan.

3 Cook the chicken in the oven alongside the vegetables for 15–18 minutes, until cooked through.

4 Serve the chicken on a bed of the roasted vegetables.

CHICKEN TIKKA MASALA

This dish is made with a great homemade curry paste that can be stored in the refrigerator for 2 weeks and used for other recipes.

SERVES 4
PREPARATION TIME 15 MINUTES
COOKING TIME 45 MINUTES

1 tablespoon coconut oil
1 onion, chopped
1 red bell pepper, cored, seeded, and sliced
4 boneless, skinless chicken breasts, about 5 oz each, cubed
1 (14½ oz) can diced tomatoes
½ cup water
2 tablespoons tomato paste
1 cup coconut milk
1 tablespoon chopped cilantro, to garnish

FOR THE CURRY PASTE
2 cardamom pods
3 garlic cloves
1 inch piece of fresh ginger root, peeled and chopped
1 red chile, seeded
1 teaspoon ground cumin
1 teaspoon ground coriander
½ teaspoon turmeric
½ teaspoon garam masala

1 To make the curry paste, remove the seeds from the cardamom pods and place in a small food processor or blender with the remaining ingredients. Blend until smooth, adding a little water to loosen, if necessary. Transfer to an airtight container and store for up to 2 weeks in the refrigerator.

2 Heat the oil in a large skillet, add the onion, and cook over low heat for 10–12 minutes, until softened and lightly golden. Stir in the red bell pepper and 2 tablespoons of the curry paste and cook for another 5 minutes.

3 Add the chicken, increase the heat, and cook for about 2 minutes, until golden, then pour in the tomatoes and measured water, add the tomato paste, and bring to a boil. Reduce the heat, cover, and simmer for 15 minutes, stirring occasionally, until the chicken is just cooked through.

4 Pour in the coconut milk and simmer for another 10 minutes. Serve sprinkled with the chopped cilantro.

CHICKEN AND BANANA KORMA

Adding bananas to a curry gives it a sweet, creamy texture.

SERVES 4
PREPARATION TIME 15 MINUTES
COOKING TIME 20–25 MINUTES

1 onion, chopped
2 garlic cloves, chopped
¾ inch piece of fresh ginger root,
   peeled and chopped
1 tablespoon olive oil
2 teaspoons mild curry powder
4 boneless, skinless chicken
   breasts, about 5 oz each, cubed
½ cup ground almonds
   (almond meal)
2 bananas, diced
1⅔ cups chicken stock
2 tablespoons slivered almonds
3 tablespoons coconut milk
freshly ground black pepper
2 tablespoons chopped cilantro,
   to garnish

1 Put the onion, garlic, and ginger in a small food processor or blender and blend to a paste.

2 Put the paste and the oil into a large skillet and cook over medium heat for 2–3 minutes. Stir in the curry powder and cook for another 3–4 minutes.

3 Add the chicken, ground almonds, bananas, and stock and bring to a boil, then reduce the heat, cover, and simmer for 10 minutes, or until the chicken is cooked through.

4 Meanwhile, heat a dry, nonstick skillet over medium-low heat and dry-fry the slivered almonds for 2–3 minutes, shaking the pan occasionally, until golden brown and toasted. Set aside.

5 Stir the coconut milk into the curry and cook for another 3–4 minutes, then season with black pepper. Sprinkle with the chopped cilantro and toasted almonds and serve.

CHICKEN AND CASHEW NUT CURRY

This rich curry could also be made with turkey if you prefer.

SERVES 4
PREPARATION TIME 15 MINUTES
COOKING TIME 25–35 MINUTES

½ cup cashew nuts
2 teaspoons cumin seeds
1 tablespoon coriander seeds
½ teaspoon fennel seeds
2 curry leaves
2 tablespoons coconut oil
4 boneless, skinless chicken
    breasts, about 5 oz each, cubed
1 onion, chopped
2 garlic cloves, crushed
¾ inch piece of fresh ginger root,
    grated
1 red chile, seeded and diced
2 cups chicken stock
1 cup fresh shredded coconut
    (or 1 cup coconut milk and
    reduce the chicken stock
    to 1 cup)
1 lb spinach leaves
freshly ground black pepper
2 tablespoons chopped cilantro,
    to garnish
steamed green vegetables,
    to serve (optional)

1 Heat a dry, nonstick skillet over medium-low heat and dry-fry the cashew nuts for 3–4 minutes, shaking the pan occasionally, until golden brown and toasted. Remove from the pan and set aside.

2 Add the seeds and curry leaves to the dry pan and dry-fry for 3–4 minutes, until fragrant, then grind in a mortar and pestle or spice grinder.

3 Heat the oil in a large skillet, add the chicken, and cook for 3–4 minutes, until browned. Add the onion, garlic, ginger, and chile and cook for another 3–4 minutes, then stir in the ground spices and continue to cook for 2–3 minutes.

4 Pour in the stock, add the coconut, and bring to a boil, then reduce the heat and simmer for 10–15 minutes, until the chicken is cooked through. Stir in the spinach and toasted cashew nuts and season with black pepper.

5 Sprinkle with the chopped cilantro and serve with steamed green vegetables, if desired.

CHICKEN CASSEROLE

••

This easy family meal, made in one dish, is ideal for a cold winter's day.

••

SERVES 4
PREPARATION TIME 10 MINUTES
COOKING TIME 1 HOUR
   10 MINUTES

1 tablespoon olive oil
1 leek, trimmed, cleaned,
   and chopped
1 celery stick, chopped
2 carrots, peeled and chopped
1 garlic clove, crushed
1 cup halved mushrooms
1 green bell pepper, cored,
   seeded, and chopped
1 tablespoon tomato paste
1¼ cups chicken stock
4 chicken thighs
4 chicken drumsticks
1 bay leaf
½ teaspoon dried marjoram
green vegetables, to serve

1 Heat the oil in a Dutch oven or flameproof casserole, add the leek, celery, carrots, and garlic, and sauté for 4–5 minutes. Add the mushrooms and green bell pepper and cook for another 4–5 minutes, until softened.

2 Stir in the tomato paste, then pour in the stock. Add the chicken pieces, bay leaf, and marjoram and bring to a simmer, then cover and cook for 1 hour, or until the chicken is tender and cooked through. Remove and discard the bay leaf.

3 Serve the casserole with your choice of green vegetables.

SPICED WALNUT CHICKEN

This dish uses spices normally associated with sweet foods, but the flavors go particularly well with the chicken and walnuts.

SERVES 2
PREPARATION TIME 10 MINUTES
COOKING TIME 30–35 MINUTES

2 tablespoons olive oil
½ cup finely chopped walnuts
¼ teaspoon chili powder
2 boneless, skinless chicken
   breasts, about 5 oz each
1 shallot, diced
½ teaspoon ground cinnamon
½ teaspoon ground nutmeg
1 cup halved grapes
juice of ½ lemon
1⅔ cups chicken stock

1 Mix together 1 tablespoon of the oil, the walnuts, and chili powder in a small bowl, then pat the mixture onto each chicken breast. Put the chicken onto a baking sheet and bake in a preheated oven, at 375°F, for 30–35 minutes, until the chicken is cooked through.

2 Meanwhile, heat the remaining oil in a skillet, add the shallot, and cook for 3–4 minutes, until softened. Add the cinnamon and nutmeg and cook for another 1–2 minutes.

3 Stir in the grapes, then pour in the lemon juice and stock and bring to a simmer. Cook for 6–8 minutes.

4 Serve the chicken with the sauce spooned over the top.

TURKEY MEATBALLS WITH ZUCCHINI TAGLIATELLE

Turkey is lean, so is a good alternative to beef or lamb. Using thigh meat helps to keep these meatballs moist.

SERVES 4
PREPARATION TIME 15 MINUTES, PLUS COOLING AND CHILLING
COOKING TIME 20–25 MINUTES

1 tablespoon olive oil
1 red onion, diced
2 garlic cloves, finely chopped
1 teaspoon ground cumin
2 teaspoons ground coriander
1 lb ground turkey
1 small bunch of cilantro
  or flat-leaf parsley,
  finely chopped
1 (14½ oz) can diced tomatoes
4 large zucchini
freshly ground black pepper

1 Heat half the oil in a skillet, add the onion, and cook for 4–5 minutes, until softened. Add the garlic and spices and season with black pepper, then cook for another 1–2 minutes. Transfer to a bowl and let cool for 5 minutes.

2 Add the turkey and chopped cilantro to the cooled onions and combine well. Shape into 16 walnut-size balls. Chill for 15 minutes.

3 Heat the remaining oil in a skillet, add the turkey balls and cook for 3–4 minutes, turning occasionally, until browning.

4 Pour in the tomatoes, bring to a simmer, and cook for another 10–12 minutes, until the meatballs are cooked through.

5 Meanwhile, cut the zucchini into thin strips, using a vegetable peeler, and cook in a saucepan of boiling water for 2–3 minutes, then drain.

6 Divide the zucchini strips among 4 warmed bowls. Spoon the turkey balls over the top and serve.

DUCK WITH BROCCOLI AND ORANGE

Duck and orange is a classic combination.

SERVES 4
PREPARATION TIME 15 MINUTES, PLUS RESTING
COOKING TIME 20–25 MINUTES

4 duck breasts, about 5 oz each
1 large head of broccoli, cut into florets
2 shallots, diced
1 red chile, seeded and finely diced
2 oranges, pith removed and segmented
freshly ground black pepper

1 Using a sharp knife, score the skin of the duck breasts in a crisscross pattern. Season with black pepper.

2 Heat an ovenproof skillet until hot, add the duck, skin side down, and cook for 7–8 minutes, until the fat runs out and the skin is golden. Turn the breasts over and cook for another 1–2 minutes, until browned. Remove 1–2 tablespoons of the duck fat and place in a separate skillet.

3 Transfer the duck to a preheated oven, at 400°F, and cook for 8–10 minutes, depending on how rare you prefer your duck.

4 Meanwhile, put the broccoli in a steamer, cover, and cook for 3–4 minutes, until tender.

5 Remove the duck from the oven. Let rest for 5 minutes.

6 While the duck is resting, heat the reserved duck fat in the pan, add the shallots and chile, and cook for 3–4 minutes, until softened. Add the steamed broccoli and toss to coat in the spicy oil, then sprinkle in the orange segments. Serve with the duck.

ROAST VENISON WITH WILD MUSHROOM SAUCE

This extravagant meal is perfect if you are entertaining dinner guests—they will never guess you are on a diet.

SERVES 4
PREPARATION TIME 10 MINUTES, PLUS RESTING
COOKING TIME 25–30 MINUTES

1 venison loin, about 1¼ lb
2 teaspoons olive oil
1 tablespoon freshly ground black pepper
4 rosemary sprigs, leaves stripped and finely chopped
8 oz wild mushrooms, cleaned
½ cup beef stock
2 teaspoons Dijon mustard
steamed carrots and green beans, to serve

1 Using a sharp knife, lightly score the skin of the venison, then rub with the oil. Sprinkle the black pepper and rosemary onto a cutting board, then rub the venison in the mixture to coat on all sides.

2 Heat a large skillet until hot, add the venison, and cook for 2 minutes on each side, or until seared. Transfer to a roasting pan and place in a preheated oven, at 400°F, for 12–15 minutes, depending on how rare you prefer your meat. Let rest for 8–10 minutes.

3 Meanwhile, cook the mushrooms in the skillet for 5–6 minutes, until softened, then pour in the stock. Bring to a boil, then reduce the heat and simmer for 10 minutes, stirring in the mustard halfway through the cooking time.

4 Carve the venison into slices and spoon the mushroom sauce over them. Serve with steamed carrots and green beans.

6

VEGETARIAN

VEGETABLE KEBABS

These kebabs work well for a barbecue, and you can use any vegetables you prefer—as long as they will stay on a skewer.

SERVES 4
PREPARATION TIME 10 MINUTES, PLUS SOAKING
COOKING TIME 10–12 MINUTES

2 tablespoons olive oil
2 tablespoons lemon juice
2 tablespoons chopped basil leaves
2 red bell peppers, cored, seeded, and chopped
1 yellow bell pepper, cored, seeded, and chopped
2 zucchini, cut into thick slices
1 large red onion, cut into wedges
freshly ground black pepper
salad greens, to serve

1 Soak 8 wooden skewers in water for at least 20 minutes to help prevent them from burning when cooking.

2 Mix together the oil, lemon juice, and basil in a bowl and season with black pepper. Put the vegetables into a large bowl, pour the marinade over them, and toss together.

3 Thread the vegetables onto the soaked skewers. Cook under a preheated medium broiler or on a barbecue grill over medium heat for 10–12 minutes, turning occasionally, until tender. Serve on salad greens.

GRILLED ASPARAGUS WITH POACHED EGG

This dish makes a satisfying lunch for one. You could also serve it as an impressive appetizer for a dinner party.

SERVES 1
PREPARATION TIME 5 MINUTES
COOKING TIME 5–7 MINUTES

10–12 asparagus spears, woody ends snapped off
1 egg
½ tablespoon olive oil
freshly ground black pepper

1 Blanch the asparagus in a saucepan of boiling water for 2 minutes. Drain, then refresh in a bowl of ice cold water and drain again. Pat dry with paper towels.

2 Poach the egg in a small saucepan of simmering water for 3–5 minutes, or until cooked to your preference.

3 Meanwhile, sprinkle the oil over the asparagus and cook in a preheated hot ridged grill pan for 3–4 minutes, until starting to char.

4 Place the asparagus on a warmed plate, top with the egg, and season with black pepper.

RATATOUILLE

A classic French dish, which is great served with broiled or grilled chicken or fish, or just on its own for vegetarians.

SERVES 4
PREPARATION TIME 15 MINUTES
COOKING TIME 35 MINUTES

4 large tomatoes
3 tablespoons olive oil
1 onion, sliced
3 garlic cloves, crushed
2 eggplants, chopped
3 zucchini, sliced
1 small bunch of basil, leaves only, coarsely torn
freshly ground black pepper

1 Put the tomatoes into a heatproof bowl and pour over enough boiling water to cover. Let stand for 1–2 minutes, then drain, cut a cross at the stem end of each tomato, and peel off the skins. Halve and seed, then set aside.

2 Heat the oil in a large skillet, add the onion and garlic, and cook for 3–4 minutes, until starting to soften. Stir in the eggplants and zucchini and cook for another 10 minutes, stirring occasionally.

3 Add the tomatoes and basil and season with black pepper. Stir well, cover, and cook for 20 minutes, until the vegetables are tender.

ASIAN MARINATED VEGETABLES

Marinating is a wonderful way of infusing a dish with loads of different flavors. You can vary the vegetables according to the season, too.

SERVES 4
PREPARATION TIME 20 MINUTES, PLUS STANDING
COOKING TIME 3–4 MINUTES

2 tablespoons sesame seeds
1 cup sugar snap peas
8 small baby corn
1 cup broccoli florets
2 carrots, peeled and cut into sticks
4 scallions, sliced
1 red bell pepper, cored, seeded, and cut into strips
½ cup bean sprouts
1 small bunch of cilantro, coarsely chopped

FOR THE DRESSING
1 garlic clove
½ inch piece of fresh ginger root, peeled
2 tablespoons lemon juice
1 teaspoon sesame oil
2 tablespoons olive oil

1 Heat a dry, nonstick skillet over medium-low heat and dry-fry the sesame seeds for 1–2 minutes, shaking the pan occasionally, until golden and toasted. Set aside.

2 Blanch the sugar snap peas, baby corn, broccoli, and carrots in a large saucepan of boiling water for 2 minutes, then drain and refresh in a bowl of ice cold water and drain again.

3 To make the dressing, place the garlic, ginger, and lemon juice in a small food processor or blender and blend together. With the motor still running, add both the oils through the feeder tube until combined.

4 Place all the blanched and raw vegetables in a large serving bowl with the cilantro. Add the dressing and toss together, then let stand for 5–10 minutes to let the flavors develop.

5 Serve sprinkled with the toasted sesame seeds.

VEGETABLE MASALA

Spice up your vegetables for a winter warming meal and, if you want even more heat, increase the amount of chili powder in the dish.

SERVES 4
PREPARATION TIME 15 MINUTES
COOKING TIME 40 MINUTES

2 garlic cloves
1 inch piece of fresh ginger root, peeled and chopped
1 (14½ oz) can diced tomatoes
½ teaspoon cayenne pepper
2 tablespoons coconut oil
1 onion, chopped
1 red bell pepper, cored, seeded, and chopped
1 yellow bell pepper, cored, seeded, and chopped
2 carrots, peeled and chopped
2 parsnips, peeled and chopped
½ teaspoon garam masala
½ teaspoon chili powder
1 small cauliflower, broken into florets
1 cup water
2 tablespoons slivered almonds, to garnish

1 Place the garlic and ginger in a small food processor or blender and blend together. Transfer to a bowl, add the tomatoes and cayenne pepper, and mix together.

2 Heat the oil in a large skillet, add the onion and bell peppers, and sauté for 8–10 minutes, until softened.

3 Stir in the carrots, parsnips, and spices and mix well, then cover and cook for 10 minutes, stirring the vegetables occasionally.

4 Add the cauliflower, tomato mixture, and measured water, bring to a simmer, and cook for 20 minutes, until all the vegetables are tender. Serve sprinkled with the slivered almonds.

7

SNACKS

BABA GANOUSH DIP WITH CRUDITÉS

This is a tasty, smoky dip that goes perfectly with crunchy vegetable sticks as a quick snack.

SERVES 4
PREPARATION TIME 10 MINUTES, PLUS COOLING
COOKING TIME 35–40 MINUTES

1 large eggplant
1 garlic clove, crushed
1 tablespoon lemon juice
1 tablespoon tahini
1½ teaspoons olive oil, plus extra if needed
½ teaspoon ground cumin
freshly ground black pepper
1 tablespoon chopped parsley, to garnish
vegetable sticks, such as carrots, bell peppers, and celery, to serve

1 Put the eggplant directly onto to an oven shelf in a preheated oven, at 400°F, and bake for 35–40 minutes, until the skin has darkened all over. Alternatively, place the eggplant over an open flame on a gas burner or barbecue grill or under a hot broiler. Let cool.

2 When cool, peel off the eggplant skin and put the flesh into a food processor or blender. Add the remaining ingredients and blend until smooth. Season with black pepper and add a little more oil, if necessary.

3 Transfer the dip to a serving bowl and sprinkle with the parsley. Serve with the crudités for dipping.

CAULIFLOWER HUMMUS

Just because you can't have chickpeas, doesn't mean you can't have hummus.

SERVES 4
PREPARATION TIME 10 MINUTES, PLUS COOLING
COOKING TIME 25 MINUTES

1 cauliflower
2 teaspoons cumin seeds
⅓ cup extra-virgin olive oil
1 garlic clove
1 tablespoon tahini
juice of 1 lemon
freshly ground black pepper

1 Break up the cauliflower into florets and cut the stem into smaller chunks. Put into a roasting pan and toss with the cumin seeds and 1 tablespoon of the oil. Put into a preheated oven, at 350°F, for 25 minutes, until tender. Let cool for 10 minutes.

2 Put the cooled cauliflower and garlic into a food processor and pulse until the mixture resembles bread crumbs. Add the tahini and lemon juice and pulse again to mix. With the motor still running, slowly add the remaining oil through the feeder tube until it forms the consistency of hummus.

3 Season with black pepper, transfer to a serving bowl, and serve.

GUACAMOLE

A Mexican classic—you can add more chile to make it hotter or blend it to make it smoother, whichever you prefer.

SERVES 2
PREPARATION TIME 10 MINUTES

1 large avocado
1 tomato, diced
juice of ½ lime
1 small bunch of cilantro leaves
½ small red onion, finely diced
½ red chile, seeded and
  finely diced
vegetable sticks, to serve

1 Halve, pit, and peel the avocado, then chop the flesh and put into a serving bowl.

2 Add the remaining ingredients and mash together with a fork to your preferred consistency.

3 Serve the guacamole with the vegetable sticks for dipping.

KALE CHIPS

• •

These are a great alternative to potato chips and far healthier. Make a large batch and serve as a snack before dinner.

• •

SERVES 4
PREPARATION TIME 10 MINUTES
COOKING TIME 12 MINUTES

1 head of kale, chopped or torn
   into large pieces
1–2 tablespoons avocado oil
freshly ground black pepper or
   other seasoning (but not salt)

1 Line a baking sheet with baking parchment.

2 Wash and thoroughly dry the kale leaves, then place them in a large bowl and toss together with the oil.

3 Place the kale on the prepared baking sheet in a single layer and bake in a preheated oven, at 350°F, for 12 minutes.

4 Remove from the oven and immediately sprinkle with black pepper or other seasoning. Let cool before serving.

SPICED NUTS AND SEEDS

These spicy nuts are handy for taking to work in a plastic container or for serving before dinner.

SERVES 6
PREPARATION TIME 5 MINUTES
COOKING TIME 13–16 MINUTES

1 tablespoon olive oil
juice of ½ lime
½ teaspoon chili powder
½ teaspoon garam masala
½ teaspoon freshly ground
    black pepper
1½ cups mixed nuts and seeds,
    such as walnuts, almonds,
    pumpkin seeds, and
    sunflower seeds
2 teaspoons honey

1 Line a baking sheet with baking parchment.

2 Whisk together the oil and lime juice in a large bowl, then slowly add the spices and black pepper, whisking to mix well.

3 Stir in the nuts and honey and mix well to thoroughly coat them with the spicy oil.

4 Spread out the nuts on the prepared baking sheet and place in a preheated oven, at 350°F, for 5–6 minutes, then toss them slightly. Return to the oven and cook for another 8–10 minutes, until the nuts and seeds start to darken.

5 Let cool on the baking sheet before serving.

NUT AND SEED CRACKERS

These crackers are perfect for serving with Guacamole (see page 118). They will keep in an airtight container for up to 5 days.

MAKES 18–20
PREPARATION TIME 10 MINUTES
COOKING TIME 40–45 MINUTES

1 cup walnuts
1 cup blanched whole almonds
3½ tablespoons ground flaxseed
3 tablespoons poppy seeds
⅓ cup unsweetened dried coconut
1 cup coarsely chopped
　savoy cabbage
2 eggs
freshly ground black pepper

1 Line a large baking sheet with baking parchment.

2 Put the walnuts and almonds into a food processor and pulse until broken down into fine crumbs. Add the flaxseed, poppy seeds, coconut, and cabbage and pulse again until the mixture forms an even consistency. Season with black pepper and add the eggs. Blend to a thick paste.

3 Spread the paste onto the paper on the prepared baking sheet. Top with another piece of baking parchment and roll out with a rolling pin until the paste is thin. Remove the top sheet of paper and cut into 18–20 squares.

4 Bake in a preheated oven, at 300°F, for 40–45 minutes, until golden. Transfer to a wire rack to cool.

SWEET POTATO WEDGES

These are delicious with one of the great dips in this book, such as Baba Ganoush (see page 116) or Cauliflower Hummus (see page 117).

SERVES 4
PREPARATION TIME 5 MINUTES
COOKING TIME 25–30 MINUTES

2 large sweet potatoes, cut into long wedges
2 tablespoons olive oil
1½ teaspoons smoked paprika
freshly ground black pepper

1 Toss the sweet potatoes with the oil, paprika, and black pepper in a large bowl, then transfer to a roasting pan.

2 Place in a preheated oven, at 400°F, for 25–30 minutes, until tender.

ZUCCHINI FRITTERS WITH POACHED EGGS

Fritters are quick and easy, and they are ideal for a packed lunch or picnic. You can replace the zucchini with corn or peas and mint.

SERVES 4
PREPARATION TIME 10 MINUTES
COOKING TIME 12–18 MINUTES

1 tablespoon olive oil
4 eggs
2 tablespoons chopped parsley, to garnish

FOR THE BATTER
1¼ cups almond flour
1 egg, beaten
⅔ cup nondairy milk
1 zucchini, diced
1 tablespoon chopped chives
freshly ground black pepper

1 To make the batter, put the flour into a large bowl and whisk in the egg and milk until smooth. Stir in the zucchini and chives and season with black pepper.

2 Heat the oil in a skillet, add tablespoons of the batter, and cook for 2–3 minutes on each side, until golden. Remove from the pan and keep warm. Repeat with the remaining batter until all the fritters are cooked.

3 Meanwhile, poach the eggs in a skillet of simmering water for 3–5 minutes, or until cooked to your preference.

4 Divide the fritters among 4 warmed plates, top with the poached eggs, and serve sprinkled with the parsley.

ROASTED PEPPERS

Roasted peppers are extremely versatile. You can fill them with vegetables, or roast them with garlic and let them cool, then slice and serve in a salad.

SERVES 4
PREPARATION TIME 10 MINUTES
COOKING TIME 25 MINUTES

2 red bell peppers, halved, cored, and seeded
2 yellow peppers, halved, cored, and seeded
1 red onion, cut into 8 wedges
18 cherry tomatoes
2 zucchini, halved and sliced
3 garlic cloves, sliced
2 tablespoons extra-virgin olive oil
1 teaspoon cumin seeds
2 tablespoons slivered almonds
freshly ground black pepper
crisp green salad, to serve

1 Put the bell pepper halves, cut side up, into a roasting pan and divide the remaining vegetables and garlic among them.

2 Sprinkle with the oil, cumin seeds, and slivered almonds and season with black pepper.

3 Roast in a preheated oven, at 400°F, for 25 minutes, until tender. Serve with a crisp green salad.

SPICED CAULIFLOWER "RICE"

Because grains are not allowed on the Paleo diet, you may want to try this "rice" alternative to serve with curries or stir-fries.

SERVES 4
PREPARATION TIME 5 MINUTES
COOKING TIME 11–14 MINUTES

1 small head of cauliflower,
   broken into florets
1 tablespoon olive oil
1 onion, finely diced
½ teaspoon turmeric
½ teaspoon cumin seeds
⅔ cup water

1 Put the cauliflower florets into a food processor and process until broken down into crumbs.

2 Heat the oil in a skillet, add the onion, and cook for 5–6 minutes, until soft. Stir in the spices, then add the cauliflower and stir well to coat.

3 Pour in the measured water, bring to a simmer, and cook for 6–8 minutes, until the cauliflower is tender.

LAMB SKEWERS

Easy to make and perfect for a summer barbecue, these lamb skewers can be made spicier by adding a diced red chile.

SERVES 2
PREPARATION TIME 10 MINUTES
COOKING TIME 6–8 MINUTES

8 oz ground lamb
½ teaspoon ground coriander
½ teaspoon ground cumin
1 garlic clove, crushed
1½ teaspoons chopped mint
1 tablespoon olive oil
crisp green salad, to serve

1 Mix together the lamb, spices, garlic, and mint in a bowl, then divide into 4 balls and shape into ovals. Thread the balls on to 2 metal skewers and brush with the oil.

2 Heat a ridged grill pan until hot, add the lamb skewers, and cook for 3–4 minutes on each side, until cooked through. Alternatively, cook the lamb skewers on a barbecue grill. Serve with a crisp green salad.

HAM OMELET ROLL

This is a great recipe if you are hungry and want to eat on the run.

SERVES 1
PREPARATION TIME 2 MINUTES
COOKING TIME 4–6 MINUTES

1 tablespoon olive oil
3 eggs
pinch of chili powder or paprika
1 slice of good-quality ham
1 scallion, shredded

1 Heat the oil in a small skillet. Beat together the eggs and chili powder or paprika in a small bowl, then pour the mixture into the pan and cook for 3–4 minutes, moving the eggs around the pan, until the bottom is set. Flip the omelet over and cook for another 1–2 minutes, until cooked through.

2 Slide the omelet onto a plate, then place the ham on top and sprinkle with the scallion. Roll up to enclose the ham and serve (or wrap in wax paper to eat later).

PROSCIUTTO-WRAPPED MELON WEDGES

This quick-and-easy snack could also be served as an appetizer for dinner.

SERVES 4
PREPARATION TIME 8 MINUTES

1 canteloupe or honeydew melon
6 slices of prosciutto, halved
   lengthwise

1 Halve, seed, and peel the melon, then cut into 12 wedges.

2 Wrap a thin slice of the prosciutto around each wedge of melon and serve—it really is that simple.

8

SWEET STUFF

BANANA AND RASPBERRY ICE CREAM

• •

This ice cream is simple to make. The banana gives it a creamy texture and you can use your favorite fruit in place of the raspberries.

• •

SERVES 2
PREPARATION TIME 15 MINUTES, PLUS FREEZING

1 banana, sliced
¾ cup raspberries
½ cup nondairy milk

1 Place the banana slices and raspberries in a single layer on a baking sheet and freeze for at least 6 hours.

2 With the motor of a food processor running, slowly drop a few slices of banana, a few raspberries, and a little of the milk into the bowl through the feeder tube. Keep adding each ingredient until the mixture forms a thick creamy ice cream. Serve immediately.

3 Alternatively, to freeze the ice cream, transfer the mixture to a freezer-proof container and place in the freezer for a few hours, then beat the mixture with a fork to prevent ice crystals from forming and making the ice cream too hard.

BANANA AND SUMMER BERRY SALAD

Summer berries and mint are a refreshing combination for a fruit salad.

SERVES 4
PREPARATION TIME 5 MINUTES, PLUS COOLING AND STANDING
COOKING TIME 1 MINUTE

juice of 1 orange
1 tablespoon honey
12–15 mint leaves, finely shredded
2 cups hulled and halved
   strawberries
2 cups blueberries
2 cups raspberries
2 large bananas, sliced

1 Put the orange juice and honey into a small saucepan and heat together until the honey is just melted. Remove from the heat and let cool, then stir in the mint.

2 Put the berries and bananas into a large bowl and pour the syrup over them. Let stand for 10 minutes before serving.

BLUEBERRY MOUSSE

A light, summery mousse, made creamier by the addition of omega-rich avocado.

SERVES 2
PREPARATION TIME 5 MINUTES,
PLUS CHILLING

1 avocado
grated zest of 1 orange
1 cup blueberries
1½ teaspoons honey
1 tablespoon ground almonds
   (almond meal)

1 Halve, pit, and peel the avocado, then coarsely chop the flesh and put into a food processor or blender with the remaining ingredients. Blend until smooth.

2 Divide between 2 glasses and chill until required.

BLUEBERRY AND ALMOND CAKE SLICES

Ground almonds are great for making rich, tasty desserts and cakes. If you only have raspberries on hand, you can use them as a substitute for the blueberries.

MAKES 9
PREPARATION TIME 10 MINUTES
COOKING TIME 22–25 MINUTES

⅓ cup coconut oil, melted, plus extra for greasing
1 cup ground almonds (almond meal)
¼ cup coconut palm sugar (jaggery) or raw sugar
½ cup coconut flour
⅓ cup blueberries
3 eggs

1 Grease a 7 inch square cake pan and line the bottom with baking parchment.

2 Put the ground almonds, sugar, flour, and blueberries into a bowl and lightly mix together.

3 Whisk together the melted oil and eggs in a small bowl, then stir into the dry ingredients. Spoon the batter into the prepared pan and smooth the top.

4 Bake in a preheated oven, at 350°F, for 22–25 minutes, until golden.

5 Cut into 9 squares, then remove from the pan and let cool on a wire rack.

WATERMELON AND STRAWBERRY SALAD

Watermelons and strawberries are best at the height of summer, when they are at their ripest.

SERVES 2
**PREPARATION TIME 5 MINUTES,
  PLUS STANDING**

¼ watermelon, peeled and cut
  into chunks
¾ cup hulled and halved
  strawberries
12 mint leaves, shredded
6 basil leaves, shredded
1 tablespoon honey

1 Mix together all the ingredients in a shallow nonmetallic bowl, then let stand for 10 minutes before serving.

PEACHES AND BERRIES WITH LIME MINT SYRUP

A great summer dish when all the fruits are readily available.

SERVES 4
PREPARATION TIME 10 MINUTES, PLUS MARINATING

4 peaches, halved, pitted, and sliced
½ cup blueberries
juice of 1 lime
2 teaspoons honey
2 tablespoons chopped mint
¾ cup raspberries
⅔ cup blackberries

1 Put the peaches, blueberries, lime juice, honey, and mint into a nonmetallic bowl and toss together. Cover and let marinate in the refrigerator for 1 hour.

2 Just before serving, toss in the raspberries and blackberries.

BAKED ALMOND AND GINGER PEACHES

Choose soft, ripe peaches for this sweet treat. You can also cook apricots or plums in the same way.

SERVES 4
PREPARATION TIME 10 MINUTES
COOKING TIME 20–22 MINUTES

2 knobs of stem ginger, diced
1 cup ground almonds
   (almond meal)
1½ tablespoons coconut oil
1 tablespoon honey
4 ripe peaches, halved and pitted

1 Mix together the ginger, ground almonds, oil, and honey in a bowl.

2 Put the peaches, cut side up, into a roasting pan. Bake in a preheated oven, at 400°F, for 10 minutes, then remove from the oven and spoon in the almond filling. Return to the oven and bake for another 10–12 minutes, until golden and soft.

3 Serve the peaches drizzled with the pan juices.

GRILLED FRUIT BROCHETTES

These are such a fun way to eat fruit—and are perfect for a summer barbecue, too.

SERVES 4
PREPARATION TIME 20 MINUTES,
** PLUS STANDING**
COOKING TIME 8–10 MINUTES

2 tablespoons honey
1 teaspoon green peppercorns
1 small bunch of mint
1 small bunch of basil
juice of 1 lime
1 cup water
1 mango, peeled and pitted
4 kiwifruit, peeled
1 pineapple, peeled and cored
8 strawberries, hulled

1 Put the honey, peppercorns, half the herbs, lime juice, and measured water into a small saucepan, bring to a boil, and boil for 1 minute. Remove from the heat and let stand for 15 minutes.

2 Meanwhile, cut all the fruit into bite-size pieces and put into a nonmetallic bowl.

3 Strain the syrup through a strainer over the fruit and let stand for at least 30 minutes (the longer you can leave it, the more intense the flavor will be).

4 Meanwhile, soak 12 small wooden skewers in water for at least 20 minutes to help prevent them from burning when cooking.

5 Thread the fruit onto the soaked skewers. Cook in a hot ridged grill pan or on a barbecue grill, for 6–8 minutes, turning frequently, until slightly caramelized. Serve with a drizzle of the remaining marinade.

MANGO BAKED APPLES

Baked apples are usually filled with rich dried fruit; these are a little lighter, but still packed full of flavor.

SERVES 4
PREPARATION TIME 20 MINUTES, PLUS STANDING
COOKING TIME 15–20 MINUTES

1 mango, peeled, pitted, and diced
grated zest and juice of 1 orange
½ cup raisins
½ cup chopped walnuts
½ teaspoon ground cinnamon
4 sweet, crisp apples

1 Put the mango and orange zest and juice into a bowl. Add the raisins and let stand for 15 minutes. Stir in the walnuts and cinnamon.

2 Core and peel the apples, then put them into a shallow ovenproof dish and spoon the mango mixture into the center of each one, pressing it down well. Pile any remaining mixture on top.

3 Bake in a preheated oven, at 350°F, for 15–20 minutes, basting once, until the apples are softened and there is plenty of juice. Serve with the juice from the pan drizzled over the top.

MANGO "CHEESECAKES"

This recipe for "cheesecake" is a good substitute for the real thing.

SERVES 4
PREPARATION TIME 15 MINUTES, PLUS COOLING AND CHILLING
COOKING TIME 10 MINUTES

½ cup ground almonds (almond meal)
1 tablespoon hazelnut butter
2 tablespoon coconut palm sugar (jaggery) or raw sugar
1 tablespoon unsweetened dried coconut
1 avocado
2 mangoes, peeled, pitted, and chopped
grated zest of 1 orange

1 Put the ground almonds and hazelnut butter into a bowl and mix together, using the back of a spoon, until the mixture resembles coarse bread crumbs. Stir in the sugar.

2 Spoon the mixture into 4 ramekins and press down evenly. Bake in a preheated oven, at 400°F, for 10 minutes. Let cool.

3 Meanwhile, heat a dry, nonstick skillet over medium-low heat and dry-fry the dried coconut, shaking the pan occasionally, until golden brown and toasted. Set aside.

4 Halve, pit, and peel the avocado, then chop the flesh and put into a food processor or blender with the mangoes and orange zest. Blend until smooth.

5 Divide the mixture among the ramekins, then sprinkle with the toasted coconut. Chill for 15 minutes before serving.

SPICY GRILLED PINEAPPLE

Pineapple is perfect for cooking in a ridged grill pan because it starts to caramelize quickly. Spicy pepper goes well with this robust fruit, or you could try black pepper as an alternative.

SERVES 4
PREPARATION TIME 5 MINUTES
COOKING TIME 13–15 MINUTES

8 slices of fresh pineapple, skin removed
3 teaspoons honey
pinch of dried red pepper flakes
pinch of ground cinnamon

1 Heat a ridged grill pan or skillet until hot, add the pineapple, and cook for 6–7 minutes on each side until starting to caramelize.

2 Add the remaining ingredients and cook until the mixture starts to simmer—this will not take long.

3 Serve the pineapple slices drizzled with the spicy honey.

CARAMELIZED FIGS WITH CASHEW CREAM

Figs don't need much doing to them to make them any more delicious, but this recipe brings out their sweetness.

SERVES 2
PREPARATION TIME 5 MINUTES
COOKING TIME 2–4 MINUTES

2 figs
2 teaspoons coconut oil
½ cup cashew nuts
⅓ cup nondairy milk
ground cinnamon, for sprinkling

1 Cut the stems off the figs, then cut in half widthwise.

2 Melt the oil in a hot ridged grill pan, add the figs, cut side down, and cook for 1–2 minutes on each side, or until starting to caramelize

3 Meanwhile, put the cashew nuts into a food processor and pulse until finely ground. With the motor still running, slowly add the milk through the feeder tube until it forms a creamy consistency

4 Remove the figs from the pan, sprinkle with cinnamon, and serve with the cashew cream.

APPLE, ALMOND, AND CINNAMON MUFFINS

These muffins are super-rich. You can also vary the recipe by adding your favorite flavors to the basic mix.

MAKES 6
PREPARATION TIME 10 MINUTES
COOKING TIME 28–30 MINUTES

1¼ cups ground almonds (almond meal)
½ cup coconut palm sugar (jaggery) or raw sugar
1 crisp, sweet apple, cored, peeled, and diced
½ teaspoon ground cinnamon
½ cup coconut oil, melted
3 eggs, beaten

1 Mix together the ground almonds, sugar, apple, and cinnamon in a bowl.

2 Whisk together the melted oil and eggs in a small bowl, then pour into the dry ingredients and mix together well. Spoon the batter into 6 sections of a muffin pan lined with muffin cups.

3 Bake in a preheated oven, at 350°F, for 28–30 minutes, until risen and golden. Remove from the pan and let cool on a wire rack.

PEAR AND ORANGE CRISP WITH ALMOND CREAM

Just because you can't have dairy, doesn't mean you can't have cream. Here, nuts and nondairy milk make an excellent cream equivalent.

SERVES 4
PREPARATION TIME 15 MINUTES
COOKING TIME 20 MINUTES

4 pears, cored and sliced
1 orange
¾ cup ground almonds (almond meal)
2 tablespoons coconut oil
pinch of ground nutmeg
2 teaspoons honey
1¼ cups blanched almonds
⅔ cup nondairy milk

1 Put the pears into a shallow ovenproof dish. Grate the zest of the orange into a separate bowl.

2 Using a sharp knife, remove the peel and pith from the orange. Holding the orange over the pears to catch the juice, cut out the segments and add to the pears.

3 Stir the ground almonds into the orange zest, then rub in the coconut oil, using the back of a spoon, until it resembles coarse bread crumbs. Stir in the nutmeg.

4 Sprinkle the crumb topping over the pears and drizzle with the honey. Bake in a preheated oven, at 400°F, for 20 minutes.

5 Meanwhile, place the blanched almonds in a food processor and pulse until finely ground. With the motor still running, gradually add the milk through the feeder tube until it forms a creamy consistency.

6 Serve the crisp warm, with the almond cream.

HONEYED TANGERINES

A slight change from caramelized oranges, tangerines have a flavor that is unique, and this recipe brings out the best in them.

SERVES 2
PREPARATION TIME 5 MINUTES
COOKING TIME 10–12 MINUTES

3 tangerines
2 tablespoons honey
1 cinnamon stick
½ cup water

1 Peel and thinly slice the tangerines, then divide the slices between 2 plates.

2 Put the honey, cinnamon stick, and measured water into a small saucepan and heat over medium heat, then simmer gently until the syrup turns golden and thickens slightly.

3 Pour the caramel over the tangerine slices and serve.

9
DRINKS

BREAKFAST SMOOTHIE

You can make a smoothie from pretty much any fruit and even some vegetables, so experiment with your favorite flavors.

SERVES 1
PREPARATION TIME 5 MINUTES

1 cup fresh or frozen mixed berries
1 small ripe banana, chopped
1 tablespoon slivered almonds
½ cup water
1 teaspoon honey (optional)

1 Put the berries, banana, slivered almonds, and measured water into a blender and blend until smooth. Add a little more water to loosen the consistency, if necessary.

2 Add honey to taste, if desired, and pour into a glass. Serve immediately.

GREEN SMOOTHIE

. . . .

This smoothie is a real health boost—add any greens you love and think of it as a refreshingly not-to-sweet summer drink.

. . . .

SERVES 1
PREPARATION TIME 5 MINUTES

1 apple
1 celery stick
¼ cucumber, chopped
½ teaspoon grated fresh
   ginger root
small handful of parsley leaves
1 small garlic clove
juice of ½ lemon
1¼ cups mineral water
freshly ground black pepper
ice cubes, to serve

1 Put all the ingredients into a blender and season with black pepper, then blend until smooth.

2 Pour over ice cubes in a glass and serve immediately.

RASPBERRY AND APPLE SMOOTHIE

Adding ground almonds to this smoothie gives it a rich, creamy consistency. Use any nondairy milk you prefer; there are now plenty to choose from.

SERVES 1
PREPARATION TIME 5 MINUTES

3 tablespoons ground almonds
½ cup raspberries
1 sweet, crisp apple, chopped
1¼ cups nondairy milk

1 Put all the ingredients into a blender and blend until smooth.

2 Pour the smoothie into a glass and serve immediately.

CREAMY COOL CUCUMBER SMOOTHIE

This green smoothie is full of goodness and tastes really fresh. You can also add any of your favorite herbs or a pinch of chili powder for a little extra punch.

SERVES 2
PREPARATION TIME 5 MINUTES

1 avocado
juice of ½ lime
⅓ cucumber, chopped
pinch of freshly ground
    black pepper
ice cubes, to serve

1 Halve, pit, and peel the avocado, then coarsely chop the flesh and put into a blender with the remaining ingredients. Blend with enough water to form a creamy, drinkable consistency.

2 Pour over ice cubes in 2 glasses and serve immediately.

APPLE AND GINGER JUICE

You will need a juicing machine to create this drink. Making your own juice is a great way of getting plenty of healthy nutrients into your body. Don't overdo the fruit, however, because it will add sugar to your diet.

SERVES 1
PREPARATION TIME 3 MINUTES

2 sweet, crisp apples
2 carrots
½ inch piece of fresh ginger root
½ lemon

1 Put all the ingredients into a juicer and process.

2 Pour into a glass and serve immediately.

SPICED ALMOND MILK

If you like drinking ice cold milk, this is the nondairy equivalent, with a touch of spice. It takes a little time to prepare, but you can make a large batch and store it in the refrigerator.

SERVES 2
PREPARATION TIME 15 MINUTES, PLUS SOAKING

1¾ cups raw almonds
3½ cups mineral or filtered water
pinch of ground cinnamon
ice cubes, to serve

1 Put the almonds into a bowl and cover with water. Let soak in the refrigerator for 24 hours.

2 Drain the almonds, then put them into a blender with the measured water and pulse until the nuts are completely broken down.

3 Put a couple of layers of cheesecloth in a strainer, then strain the milk into a small bowl, squeezing out the excess moisture from the almonds.

4 Pour over ice cubes in 2 glasses, sprinkle with cinnamon, and serve immediately.

ICED MINT TEA

Green tea is rich in antioxidants and has been shown to have many health benefits. Make a pitcher of this refreshing iced tea for those days when you need a thirst quencher.

SERVES 4–6
PREPARATION TIME 2 MINUTES,
PLUS COOLING AND CHILLING

handful of mint leaves
3–4 green tea bags
4 cups boiling water
honey (optional)
ice cubes, to serve

1 Gently bruise half the mint leaves and put them into a heatproof bowl.

2 Add the tea bags and pour over the measured water. Cover and let cool, then chill for 3–4 hours.

3 Remove the tea bags and mint, then stir in the remaining mint leaves and a little honey, if desired.

4 Pour over ice cubes in glasses and serve immediately.

MANGO AND FLAXSEED SMOOTHIE

Ground flaxseeds are a great source of omega-3 essential fats, and they also help to support the detoxification process, which is important if you are trying to lose weight.

SERVES 1
PREPARATION TIME 5 MINUTES

1 ripe mango, peeled, pitted, and chopped
⅔ cup nondairy milk
2 teaspoons ground flaxseed
½ teaspoon honey (optional)
ice cubes, to serve

1 Put the mango, milk, and flaxseeds into a blender and blend until smooth. Add the honey to taste, if desired.

2 Pour over ice cubes in a glass and serve immediately.

INDEX

A

alcohol 18

almonds
  almond cream 143
  apple, almond, and cinnamon muffins 142
  baked almond and ginger peaches 136
  blueberry and almond cake slices 133
  spiced almond milk 151
  tomato, saffron, and almond soup 36

apples
  apple, almond, and cinnamon muffins 142
  apple and ginger juice 150
  mango baked apples 138
  pork, apple, and sage burgers with honeyed onions 95
  raspberry and apple smoothie 148

arugula
  leek and arugula soup 31
  arugula pesto 38

Asian marinated vegetables 113

Asian salad 39

asparagus
  dippy egg with asparagus spears 25
  grilled asparagus with poached egg 111

avocados
  avocado salsa 57
  blueberry mousse 132
  chilled avocado soup with red pepper salsa 34–35
  crab and avocado salad 40
  creamy cool cucumber smoothie 149
  guacamole 118
  mango and avocado salsa 80
  mango "cheesecakes" 139
  orange, avocado ,and cashew salad 53
  shrimp, watermelon, and avocado salad 41

B

baba ganoush dip with crudités 116

bacon
  breakfast tortilla 23
  summer veggies and eggs with crispy bacon 98

bananas
  banana and raspberry ice cream 130
  banana and summer berry salad 131
  breakfast banana split 26
  breakfast smoothie 146
  chicken and banana korma 102

beans 17

beef
  Moroccan beef kebabs 86
  spicy beef stir-fry 87
  steak with mushroom and red wine sauce 89
  tenderloin steak with sweet potato fries 88

beets: roasted beet, watercress, and orange salad 48

bell peppers
  chilled avocado soup with red pepper salsa 34–35
  broiled cod with peperonata 66
  huevos rancheros 22
  lemon pork and mixed pepper kebabs 96
  roasted 124

berries
  banana and summer berry salad 131

breakfast smoothie 146
peaches and berries with lime mint
    syrup 135
blueberries
    blueberry and almond cake slices 133
    blueberry mousse 132
breakfast banana split 26
breakfast smoothie 146
breakfast tortilla 23
broccoli: duck with broccoli and
    orange 107
brochettes, grilled fruit 137
burgers, pork, apple, and sage 95
butternut squash, baked pork chops with
    fennel and 94

C

cabbage, coconut 59
Caesar salad, shrimp 42
cakes: apple, almond, and cinnamon
    muffins 142
    blueberry and almond cake slices 133
carpaccio, tuna 73
cashew nuts
    cashew cream 141
    chicken and cashew nut curry 103
    crispy duck and cashew salad 45
    orange, avocado, and cashew salad 53
casseroles
    chicken casserole 104
cauliflower
    cauliflower hummus 117
    spiced cauliflower "rice" 125
ceviche, salmon and grapefruit 58
chicken
    chicken and banana korma 102
    chicken and cashew nut curry 103
    chicken casserole 104
    chicken packages with roasted
        ratatouille 99
    chicken tikka masala 100–1

honey and mustard chicken salad 44
    spiced walnut chicken 105
chiles
    chili oil 61
    mussels in spicy tomatoes 78
    red pepper salsa 34–35
chips, kale 119
chorizo and egg-topped baked
    mushrooms 21
chowder, smoked haddock and corn 29
coconut cabbage 59
cod
    broiled cod with peperonata 66
    broiled cod with pesto and green
        beans 65
    orange and tomato roasted cod 64
    pan-fried cod with minted pea
        puree 63
coleslaw
    fennel 71
    ginger and orange mackerel with
        coleslaw 70
    ginger, snow pea, and bean sprout
        coleslaw 54
corn: smoked haddock and corn
    chowder 29
crab
    crab and avocado salad 40
    crab and sweet potato cakes 79
crackers, nut and seed 121
crisp, pear and orange 143
cucumber
    creamy cool cucumber
        smoothie 149
    gazpacho 33
    mango and avocado salsa 80
curries
    chicken and banana korma 102
    chicken and cashew nut curry 103
    chicken tikka masala 100–1
    mackerel 68–69

Thai green shrimp curry 82–83
vegetable masala 114

D

dairy products 16, 18
dips
    baba ganoush dip with crudités 116
    cauliflower hummus 117
    guacamole 118
duck
    crispy duck and cashew salad 45
    duck with broccoli and orange 107

E

eggplants
    baba ganoush dip with crudités 116
    ratatouille 99, 112
eggs
    baked eggs with spinach and ham 24
    breakfast tortilla 23
    chorizo and egg-topped baked
        mushrooms 21
    dippy egg with asparagus spears 25
    grilled asparagus with poached egg 111
    ham omelet roll 127
    huevos rancheros 22
    shrimp and egg stir-fry 84
    smoked haddock scrambled eggs 20
    summer veggie and eggs with crispy
        bacon 98
    zucchini fritters with poached
        eggs 123
exercise 11

F

fennel
    baked pork chops with fennel and
        butternut squash 94
    broiled red snapper and roasted fennel
        with chili oil 61
    mackerel fillets with fennel coleslaw 71

figs
    caramelized figs 141
    fig and ham salad 43
fish
    fish stew 76
    fish tagine 74–75
    see also cod, mackerel, etc.
food diaries 15
fritters, zucchini 123
fruit 17
    broiled fruit brochettes 137
    see also individual types of fruit

G

gazpacho 33
ginger
    apple and ginger juice 150
    baked almond and ginger peaches
        136
    ginger and orange mackerel with
        coleslaw 70
    ginger, snow pea, and bean sprout
        coleslaw 54
grapefruit: salmon and grapefruit
    ceviche 58
green beans: pesto beans 65
guacamole 118

H

haddock
    smoked haddock and corn
        chowder 29
    smoked haddock scrambled eggs 20
ham
    baked eggs with spinach and ham
        24
    fig and ham salad 43
    ham omelet roll 127
health benefits 10
horseradish: salmon and horseradish
    soup 28

huevos rancheros 22
hummus, cauliflower 117

I
ice cream, banana and raspberry 130
iced mint tea 152
Indian salad, crunchy 49

J
juice, apple and ginger 150

K
kale
  crunchy kale salad 52
  kale chips 119
kebabs
  lemon pork and mixed pepper 96
  Moroccan beef 86
  vegetable 110
korma, chicken and banana 102

L
lamb
  lamb and rosemary stew 92
  lamb skewers 126
  Moroccan rack of lamb 91
leek and arugula soup 31
lemons
  lemon and parsley sardines 72
  lemon pork and mixed pepper
    kebabs 96
liver: grilled liver with mashed sweet
  potatoes 90

M
mackerel
  ginger and orange mackerel with
    coleslaw 70
  mackerel curry 68–69
  mackerel fillets with fennel
    coleslaw 71

snow peas: ginger, snow pea, and bean
  sprout coleslaw 54
mangoes
  mango and avocado salsa 80
  mango and flaxseed smoothie 153
  mango baked apples 138
  mango "cheesecakes" 139
meatballs: turkey meatballs with zucchini
  tagliatelle 106
melon: prosciutto-wrapped melon
  wedges 128
milk substitutes 18
mint
  iced mint tea 152
  minted pea puree 63
  peaches and berries with lime mint
    syrup 135
monkfish, pancetta-wrapped 62
Moroccan beef kebabs 86
Moroccan rack of lamb 91
mousse, blueberry 132
muffins, apple, almond, and cinnamon 142
mushrooms
  chorizo and egg-topped baked
    mushrooms 21
  mushroom and spinach-stuffed pork
    tenderloin 93
  mushroom-stuffed trout 67
  roast venison with wild mushroom
    sauce 108
  steak with mushroom and red wine
    sauce 89
mussels
  mussels in spicy tomatoes 78
  seafood stir-fry 81

N
nuts
  nut and seed crackers 121
  spiced nuts and seeds 120
  see also almonds, etc.

O

oils 17
omelets: ham omelet roll 127
onions
  onion soup 32
  pork, apple, and sage burgers with
    honeyed onions 95
oranges
  duck with broccoli and orange 107
  ginger and orange mackerel with
    coleslaw 70
  orange and tomato roasted cod 64
  orange, avocado, and cashew salad 53
  pear and orange crisp with almond
    cream 143
  roasted beet, watercress, and
    orange salad 48
organic food 16

P

Paleo tabbouleh 51
pancetta
  broiled pancetta-wrapped radicchio 97
  pancetta-wrapped monkfish 62
parsnips: Paleo tabbouleh 51
pea puree: pan-fried cod with minted 63
peaches
  baked almond and ginger peaches 136
  peaches and berries with lime mint
    syrup 135
peanuts 18
pear and orange crisp with almond
  cream 143
pesto
  arugula pesto 38
  pesto beans 65
pineapple, spicy grilled 140
pork
  baked pork chops with fennel and
    butternut squash 94
  lemon pork and mixed pepper
    kebabs 96
  mushroom and spinach-stuffed pork
    tenderloin 93
  pork, apple, and sage burgers with
    honeyed onions 95
pregnancy, and the Paleo diet 16
prosciutto-wrapped melon wedges 128

R

radicchio, broiled pancetta-wrapped 97
raspberries
  banana and raspberry ice cream 130
  raspberry and apple smoothie 148
ratatouille 112
  chicken packages with roasted
    ratatouille 99
red snapper: broiled red snapper and
  roasted fennel with chili oil 61
rosemary: lamb and rosemary stew 92

S

salads 37–54
  Asian 39
  banana and summer berry 131
  chunky cumin Waldorf 50
  coleslaw 70
  crab and avocado 40
  crispy duck and cashew 45
  crunchy Indian 49
  crunchy kale 52
  fig and ham 43
  ginger, snow pea, and bean sprout
    coleslaw 54
  honey and mustard chicken 44
  orange, avocado, and cashew 53
  Paleo tabbouleh 51
  shrimp Caesar 42
  shrimp, watermelon, and avocado 41
  roasted beet, watercress, and
    orange 48

spinach and salmon 38
superfood 46–47
watermelon and strawberry 134
salmon
  broiled salmon with avocado salsa 57
  broiled salmon with coconut
    cabbage 59
  honey and wasabi-glazed salmon
    fillets 56
  salmon and grapefruit ceviche 58
  salmon and horseradish soup 28
  spinach and salmon salad with arugula
    pesto 38
salsa
  avocado 57
  mango and avocado 80
  red pepper 34–35
sardines, lemon and parsley 72
sauces
  mushroom and red wine 89
  wild mushroom 108
scallops: spicy seared scallops with
  mango and avocado salsa 80
sea bass: Thai sea bass packages 60
seafood stir-fry 81
seeds
  nut and seed crackers 121
  spiced nuts and seeds 120
sesame-seared tuna with Asian
    salad 39
shrimp
  shrimp and egg stir-fry 84
  shrimp Caesar salad 42
  shrimp, watermelon, and avocado
    salad 41
  Thai green shrimp curry 82–83
skewers, lamb 126
smoked haddock
  smoked haddock and corn
    chowder 29
  smoked haddock scrambled eggs 20

smoothies
  breakfast 146
  creamy cool cucumber smoothie 149
  green 147
  mango and flaxseed 153
  raspberry and apple 148
snacks 18, 115–28
soups 27–36
  chilled avocado 34–35
  gazpacho 33
  leek and arugula 31
  onion 32
  roasted tomato and garlic 30
  salmon and horseradish 28
  smoked haddock and corn
    chowder 29
  tomato, saffron, and almond 36
spinach
  baked eggs with spinach and
    ham 24
  chicken and cashew nut curry 103
  mushroom and spinach-stuffed pork
    tenderloin 93
  spinach and salmon salad with arugula
    pesto 38
squash, baked pork chops with fennel and
    butternut 94
squid with tomatoes 77
stews
  fish 76
  fish tagine 74–75
  lamb and rosemary 92
stir-fries
  seafood 81
  shrimp and egg 84
  spicy beef 87
strawberries: watermelon and strawberry
    salad 134
summer veggies and eggs with crispy
    bacon 98
superfood salad 46–47

sweet potatoes
    crab and sweet potato cakes 79
    grilled liver with mashed sweet
      potatoes 90
    sweet potato wedges 122
    tenderloin steak with sweet potato
      fries 88
syrup, lime mint 135

T

tabbouleh, Paleo 51
tagine, fish 74–75
tangerines, honeyed 144
tea, iced mint 152
Thai green shrimp curry 82–83
Thai sea bass packages 60
tomatoes
    gazpacho 33
    huevos rancheros 22
    mussels in spicy tomatoes 78
    orange and tomato roasted cod 64
    ratatouille 112
    roasted tomato and garlic soup 30
    squid with tomatoes 77
    tomato, saffron, and almond soup 36
tortilla, breakfast 23
trout, mushroom-stuffed 67
tuna
    sesame-seared tuna with Asian
      salad 39
    tuna carpaccio 73
turkey meatballs with zucchini
    tagliatelle 106

V

vegans 10, 16
vegetables
    Asian marinated vegetables 113
    vegetable kebabs 110
    vegetable masala 114
vegetarian dishes 10, 16, 109–14

venison: roast venison with wild mushroom
    sauce 108

W

Waldorf salad, chunky cumin 50
walnuts: spiced walnut chicken 105
watercress: roasted beet, watercress, and
    orange salad 48
watermelon
    shrimp, watermelon, and avocado
      salad 41
    watermelon and strawberry salad 134
weight loss 17
wild mushroom sauce, roast venison
    with 108

zucchini
    zucchini fritters with poached
      eggs 123
    turkey meatballs with zucchini
      tagliatelle 106